"Help! I Just Pulled my Kids Out of School"

Guidance From 17 Years of Homeschooling

Nina Elena

ZAMIZ PRESS

Nonfiction > Family & Relationships > Education

Education & Reference > Education > Home Schooling

Special discounts are available on quantity purchases by corporations, associations and others. For details contact the author.

DO YOU HAVE A MESSAGE TO SHARE WITH THE WORLD? ARE YOU INTERESTED IN HAVING YOUR BOOK PUBLISHED? VISIT ZAMIZPRESS.COM

No part of this publication may be reproduced, distributed or transmitted in any form or by any means, including photocopying, recording, or other electronic or mechanical methods, without the prior written permission of the publisher, except in the case of brief quotations embodied in critical reviews and certain other noncommercial uses permitted by copyright law.

Copyright © 2023 Nina Elena. All rights reserved.

Cover Design: Nathaniel Dasco

Editing: Rebecca Black

"Help! I Just Pulled my Kids out of School" Guidance from 17 Years of Homeschooling / Nina Elena

ISBN: 978-1-949813-33-3, 978-1-949813-34-0, 978-1-949813-32-6

Contents

1. I'M BEGINNING TO PANIC — 1
   What Have I Done? — 3
   What is Real Homeschooling? — 3
   Is it Worth it? — 5
   Are all Homeschoolers the Same? — 10

2. HOW DO I GET STARTED? — 17
   Homeschooling is Legal, Right? — 17
   Why Should I Homeschool? — 18
   Should I Have a Schedule or be More Relaxed? — 21
   What Does a Homeschool Day Look Like? — 21

3. ARE THERE DIFFERENT WAYS TO HOMESCHOOL? — 31
   Traditional Method — 32
   Charlotte Mason Method — 32
   Unschooling — 33
   Charter Schools — 35
   Classical Education — 40
   Pods — 42
   What is a Co-op? — 43

4. I THINK I'M IN, NOW WHAT? — 45
   How do I Pick Curriculum? — 45
   Are Homeschool Kids in the Same Grade Level as Public School? — 55
   Should I Buy New or Used Books? — 57
   Which Things Make Homeschooling Easier? — 62

Are There any Curriculums You
Recommend? 65
How Much Does it Cost to Homeschool? 71

5. SHOULD MY HOUSE LOOK LIKE A
SCHOOL? 75
How do I Create a "Learning Environment"? 75
Are There Community Resources for
Homeschoolers? 83
What is a Homeschool Convention? 83

6. HOW CAN I MAKE SURE MY HOMESCHOOL
IS SUCCESSFUL? 85
Are You Saying You Run Your Home Like a
Business? 85
How Can I Know if I'm Doing it Right? 88
What Can I do While Waiting for my
Materials to Arrive? 90
What is Deschooling? 90

7. BUT AREN'T HOMESCHOOLED KIDS
UNCOOL? 93
What About Socialization? 93
If I Build it, Will They Come? 95

8. HOW DO I HANDLE HARD DAYS? 97
How do I Respond When Someone Objects
to Homeschool? 102
How do I Homeschool Multiple Kids at the
Same Time? 104
Can I Homeschool my Child with Special
Needs? 105
Will I Ever Have "Me Time" Again? 107
What if my Child Can't Focus? 109
What if I Only Have One Child? 111
What do I Teach at Each Stage? 112

9. IS IT POSSIBLE TO HOMESCHOOL MY
HIGH SCHOOLER? 115
   What Challenges Does High School
   Present? 115
   How do I Create a High School Plan? 118
   Can my Kids Officially Graduate and go to
   College? 120

10. WHAT ELSE DO I NEED TO KNOW? 123
   How Can I Learn from Your Mistakes? 126

11. PREVIEW OF THE NEXT BOOK, "HELP! I
NEED SOME HOMESCHOOL TIPS" 129

   Afterword: Can You Just Tell me What
   to do? 133
   About the Author 141
   Recommended Reading 143
   Endnotes 145
   Editor's Note 151

Chapter 1

I'm Beginning to Panic

Today's the day. You just left your son's school, shaking. He is not going back. Now the gnawing doubt is starting to grow. You know you've done the right thing, but as you drive home, your eyes are wide with fear. Your mind starts racing. "What have I done? Can I really do this? What if it doesn't work out? Will he have any friends? I'm in over my head!"

Take a deep breath, hold it for a second, now slowly let it out.

You're going to be all right. Your child is going to be more than all right. And in a year, you'll look back on this day and chuckle at how scared you were. By the end of this book, you will know all about homeschooling. You'll know the legalities, the lingo and just what to do in each circumstance. By this time next year, you could be helping a new homeschool mom who looks to *you* as the expert!

While you're reading this, put on a movie for your kids that shows homeschooling in a positive light. Three great movies are *RV*, starring Robin Williams, *Mom's Night Out*, starring Sean Astin, and *Courageous*, starring Alex Kendrick.

Hold your head up. You've just made an incredibly brave decision, and I'm so proud of you.

Today I will introduce you to people, books and resources that will give you the tools you need for success, one of these people is Vicki Bentley.

Vicki is a rockstar in the homeschool community. She makes it look effortless, which is a testimony to how much effort she put in. While I have homeschooled for 17 years, Vicki has homeschooled 17 children. She brings a special wisdom and perspective. She is the mother of eight daughters and has also been a foster mom to over fifty children. Now she is a grandmother to 23 grandchildren and 10 great-grandchildren. She has addressed state and national homeschool conventions, as well as speaking to university teacher organizations.

Look for Vicki's homeschool insights in her "Vicki Says" segments that begin with her picture and end with this ∼ symbol.

Throughout this book I will share factual information, as well as insights and ideas. The ideas I share and the personal examples I give are not meant to tell you exactly what to do. My hope is that they will get you thinking about ways to create your own versions that are unique to your family. I can tell you what's worked for us, but my goal is to inspire you, not to boss you around.

What Have I Done?

Is one of your concerns that your child won't be at the same educational level as their public-school friends?

When moments of doubt creep into your mind, remember these statistics. In 2022, 93% of Baltimore students in third through eighth grade tested below grade level in math. 23 of those Baltimore schools didn't have a single child test at grade level[1]. Not one.

Across the country a 13-year-old Ukrainian refugee asked to return to war ravaged Ukraine, rather than stay in the dangerous San Francisco school she attended[2].

The San Francisco Examiner reported in January that another school had, "students recording videos of themselves as they beat another student, three female students assaulting a special-education student, and a student bringing an air gun to school—all without documented suspensions at the time of those incidents."[3]

You've made a great choice.

What is Real Homeschooling?

When I talk about homeschooling, I mean giving your children a comprehensive education at home. This might also be called traditional homeschooling. It includes teaching the four core subjects of **math, history,**

language arts, and **science.** In high school, it would also include other subjects called "electives".

I am not referring to virtual learning, take home packets, home instruction due to chronic illness or pandemic learning. Those are not homeschooling.

We will talk about other methods of homeschooling in chapter 3. For now, I just want you to understand how I use the word homeschool.

One of the most common questions new homeschooling parents ask is, "Am I qualified to homeschool my children?" There are successful homeschool parents who are high school dropouts or who barely speak the language. Some homeschooling moms have chronic illnesses and teach school from bed while friends bring their child on field trips. There are also homeschool parents who are molecular biologists, doctors, EMTs and lawyers. Where there's a will, there's a way. Any parent who loves their children enough to research how to homeschool them and then does what is necessary to educate their children, is qualified.

Today, take time to look online for meetups, support groups, classes and park play days for your kids. Find and start going to these before you're in desperate need of social time and even before you feel ready. The day is coming when both you and your children will desperately need the support of people who are swimming upstream from the culture to have a better life. You will need the encouragement from other moms, and your children will need the camaraderie and laughter of other kids.

As you begin your journey into homeschooling, let me

advise you to listen to people who have already accomplished what you want to accomplish. Find those who have graduated successful adult children, have a strong marriage, have healthy living habits, a friendly attitude, and those who seem normal. Don't emulate someone who isn't living a life you want to copy.

When I began homeschooling our children, I sought advice and mentorship from people who had been homeschooling for long enough to graduate some of their children. I wanted to see the finished product. Had anyone been doing this long enough to have adult children who were successful and well-rounded?

Is it Worth it?

There are many stories of homeschool families with children who graduated college with a bachelor's degree in physics at age 13, such as Elliott Tanner. He is now pursuing his PhD. Elliot enrolled in college at age 9.

Another family, Kip and Mona Lisa Harding, have ten children and each has graduated high school by the age of 12.

In fact, many Ivy league universities are actively recruiting homeschooled students due to their knowledge, intelligence, and ability to work independently.

"'The high achievement level of homeschoolers is readily recognized by recruiters from some of the best colleges in the nation,' said Dr. Susan Berry, who researches and writes about educational topics like the fast-growing rate of homeschooling. 'Schools such as Massachusetts Institute of Technology, Harvard, Stanford, and Duke University all actively recruit homeschoolers.'"[4]

Some homeschool graduates forgo college and turn their high school side business into full-time entrepreneurship. Others take their high school apprenticeships and become full-time skilled labor, making forty dollars an hour.

    Homeschool terms:
        Arithmetic= math
        History= United States history or world history
        Science= understanding the natural world, the scientific method and how the body works
        Language arts= reading, spelling, sentence structure (nouns, verbs, periods, commas)
        Electives= optional classes such as a foreign language, music, drama, robotics, art, logic, etc.

My goal for our children was to have them graduate high school with all the skills they would need to support themselves in the adult world. What they decided to do with their adult lives would be their decision. Besides a great education, I wanted them to have good financial knowledge, the ability to write well, great interpersonal skills, a willingness to learn, and one entire skill-set they could monetize. I choose the skill set based on their strengths. Our oldest excelled in writing and loved to organize. She would make the perfect executive assistant. That meant her electives were in Microsoft Word, Office,

Excel, and PowerPoint. When she graduated, she was fully qualified to walk into any office and get a position.

Our son had different strengths, so by the time he graduated high school, his strengths in robotics, electronics, communication, and arithmetic, prepared him to walk into any technical industry and talk his way into a position.

Both of our older children attended community college on-campus while in high school. This allowed them the opportunity to see the college atmosphere in small snippets and to graduate from high school with college credits.

I loved hearing the stories they told of college professors asking them, "How do you know so much? Were you homeschooled?"

Some affirmed them with, "You're the only one who is paying attention in class." Or, "You're my best student!"

It was validating to hear that our commitment to education and personal responsibility made them stand out in a college classroom of high school graduates and older adult students.

An early introduction to college gave our kids confidence in their abilities. They both had lots of friends throughout their homeschool years and made many more at college. I am constantly amazed at their mental strength and character. Are they perfect? No. But neither are we. We are incredibly proud of the people they have become and have never looked back on a single day of homeschooling and regretted our decision.

How you decide to homeschool is a personal decision. As Jordan Peterson says, "You're going to pay a price for every bloody thing you do and everything you don't do. You don't get to choose to not pay a price. You get to choose which poison you're going to take. That's it."[5]

Even with good intentions, we are each going to make mistakes and those mistakes will cost us. But when we look back at our decisions, we can judge them based on two criteria:

1. Did we make the best decision we could with the information we had at the time?

2. Did we do what was best and stick with it when it got hard? Or did we give up and do what was easy?

As Zig Ziglar says, "I'll do today what other people won't, so I can have tomorrow what other people can't."[6]

Parenting is hard and homeschool parenting is even harder, but the rewards are endless.

Each person walks into homeschooling with their own set of issues to overcome. Your life will change, your free time will change and where you put your focus will change. You will need to brush up on child psychology, stages of development, and learning styles.

There are also preconceived notions we each carry around. You may have to drop the wall you've put up to protect yourself from catty moms at the pickup line with their fancy coffees and designer handbags.

Homeschool moms come in all shapes and sizes. Some hike with their kids, some buy things at Walmart, and many don't always wear makeup. Some make a lot of money and hire private tutors. Others have no money and make their curriculum from scratch just like they make their bread.

Homeschooling is the great equalizer. It's a very diverse bunch of families who have one goal in mind, the best for their children. If you spend enough time with them, you will find someone in the group you click with. You will also find someone who is a great mentor. One day a mom who is even more scared than you are today will walk in and you'll be the expert she looks up to. You will find your place. It just takes time.

A good place to start is with a set of goals. Let's put our heads together to create a list of goals for your children. Today write down:

1. Your life goals for your children

(Example: I want my children to know enough to succeed in any situation, know how to learn what they don't know, be kind to others, be strong leaders and share Jesus with others.)

2. Your educational goals for your children

(Example: My children will have an extensive knowledge of _____ [maybe language or science or history]. They will have a firm grasp of _____ [maybe math or reading or Spanish]. And they will know enough _____ (language/science/ math/ history) not to feel stupid.

3. A family motto

(Example: "To go where no man has gone before" -Star Trek)

4. In a perfect world, what would you want for your children?

Are all Homeschoolers the Same?

Our priorities have always been for our children to 1. become strong readers; 2. be excellent communicators; 3. have a working knowledge of math and science; 4. have a love of history; and 5. use logic and critical thinking to analyze information. Why? Because we knew that if they could read with ease, they could learn anything. Understanding the world around them is important. Without math skills, they could be easily overcharged and unable to manage their own finances or business. They should also be able to communicate effectively with others in business and life. If they knew history well, they would be able to notice when history tries to repeat itself. And if they could think logically and critically about information, they would be able to see through lies.

If we were a family of engineers, perhaps our focus would be different. If we were artists or biologists, they might also be different.

There's no need to be like everyone else. Homeschoolers are an eclectic bunch.

Homeschool groups are usually very diverse. One mom wears flowing dresses and flowers in her hair while another wears yoga pants and a weave. Some families eat takeout every day and some grind their own organic wheat. It's not unusual to see a mom with blue hair laughing together with a mom in a hijab. If you can think it, there's a homeschool family to represent it and all the kids are playing together. It's a beautiful sight.

When our children graduated high school and headed to college, they needed to know how to read well and use the library for research. That way, if they make bad career choices or if the job market takes a turn for the worse, they can learn anything by reading about it. I thought that if they were excellent readers, they would have the ability to study for a new career. If the world experiences a zombie apocalypse and all electronics are gone, they can break into an abandoned library and learn any skill they need. We gave them the tools to accomplish anything. If we didn't give them the tools, they would struggle just to survive everyday life. Why would we want that for them?

As much as I love homeschooling, it surprises most moms to hear that I didn't homeschool willingly. One day my husband came to me and said that since we were going to move, I should investigate homeschooling. I was not thrilled with the idea, to put it mildly. But he was right, we were about to move and that would have meant our oldest would have spent one month in her current school. Then she would have been in a new school for a month as we lived with family while house hunting. Finally, she would have been in a third school once we bought a house. That sounded very stressful for a first grader.

My first thought was that homeschool families were weird and that I wasn't about to wear jean dresses and head coverings, so I wouldn't fit in. I'm not sure where I got that idea from, but that was my thinking.

Our pastor's family and the assistant pastor's family both homeschooled their kids. They were normal, happy families and their adult children were fantastic. I called one woman and arranged a time to go to her house. I walked in and said, "Okay, show me what this homeschooling thing is all about."

She pulled out her youngest child's schoolbooks and I was in awe. I had never seen such great school materials. I'd spent time in our oldest child's kindergarten classroom and had observed the level of instruction and materials. These homeschool materials were a thousand times better. The quality of the books, the information and the graphics made the sloppily copied papers that came home each week look like garbage. I was hooked. My child could get this level of education, a private school education, and I could do it from home at a fraction of the cost!

I immediately ordered the Abeka catalog and couldn't wait to go through it. I will explain the first mistake I made with this in chapter 10.

There was one other reservation I had about homeschooling. We have very high expectations for our children. We see how smart they are and want them to live up to their potential. Could I have the patience to teach them without being overbearing and crushing their spirits? God gave me my answer a few weeks later.

It was time for our oldest child's school assembly, and I sat on the bleachers as the classes came in. One teacher stood out as she berated the children in her class for having a foot over the line or wiggling while waiting. She was particularly harsh with her class of third graders. In that moment, I knew that even if I was too strict or expected too much from my kids, at least it would come from a place of love. My error would be that I loved them too much to let them be less than they could be. That was a potential problem I could live with.

Our daughter's first grade curriculum was ordered along with some preschool workbooks for our son, and we began our journey into homeschooling!

Three months into our journey, we settled into our new home. My husband asked when I was going to enroll our oldest in school. It was too late. We absolutely loved homeschooling and our local homeschool group, so we decided to stick with it. By the end of that first year, we all loved the homeschool life and never looked back.

Vicki Says:

Homeschooling is more than simply "school at home." It's not even really an education choice—it's a lifestyle choice. Homeschooling is just one aspect of *home discipleship*. The Greek model of education was founded on pursuit of knowledge, but the Hebrew model of education was founded on pursuit of relationship.[1] I encourage you to connect with your child, to convey to him that your love for him is not dependent upon how fast he can finish his math work or how many science experiments he does a week.

Another second-generation homeschool mom has gradually grown to appreciate–after becoming a mom herself–the good intentions of her own imperfect parents and the benefits of homeschooling, even though she balked at cooperating in middle school and even the teen years.

"The thinking behind my refusing to do school during that time? I'm pretty sure it was mostly stubborn rebellion. Taking a stand against my mom personally and trying to give her as hard a time as possible as our relationship deteriorated."

But she also introspectively notes, when asked what her mom could have done differently:

"I think somehow, she missed the mark on finding a way to truly connect with me and act towards me in a way that made me feel seen and heard and understood while I was younger... and then that chance passed for us as I started turning into a teenager and developing rebellious habits and attitude so that she had to address all of that junk instead of focusing on building a better connection.

So, I think the key to a successful homeschool relationship with your child is to absolutely make sure that you are building that *emotional and personal connection* way before and throughout the actual schoolwork process. I just feel like we never hit that connection properly and the rest fell apart from there..."

Thankfully, she and her mom are now working on restoring the lost years.

Life is messy. Homeschooling isn't the answer to all your family's problems.[2] Folks, it doesn't matter if your kids can solve quadratic equations–if they can hardly wait to get out of your house, and then don't ever want to talk to you again. Build connections. I wasn't a very joyful mom for quite a few years, but eventually realized I had allowed God's enemy to rob me of my joy. So, I had to be purposeful about building connections with my kids, about "tying love-strings" from my heart to theirs.[3] I encourage you to be intentional.

WHEN YOU HAVE time to sit down and figure out which brands of curriculum to buy for each subject, be sure to pick things that excite you and you think will work well for your kids. Teaching is often a transference of feeling from one person to another. In homeschooling that means that if you're fascinated by history or math, teach that to your children. Your enthusiasm will rub off and they will enjoy it as well because you made it come alive. But if you absolutely hate a subject, that can come across as well. That's not a feeling you want to transfer. So that would be a great subject to farm out to an online course or a local in-person class.

If you feel that way about every subject, then it's probably time to sit down and think about some more serious things, like the questions at the beginning of this chapter. You're going to have to roll up your sleeves and do some deep work on yourself and your family. But after you've gone through that work, you will see beautiful changes.

There is a learning curve to staying home with your children.

I have broken everything in this book into chapters, but I suggest even reading chapters that don't apply to your situation. There may be a tip or trick you'll miss if you skip that section.

Chapter 2

How do I Get Started?

Homeschooling is Legal, Right?

"Homeschooling has been legal throughout the United States for about 25 years, but regulations vary dramatically by state. Only two states require background checks for parents who choose to homeschool, and just ten require parents to have a high school degree. Fewer than half require any kind of evaluation or testing of homeschooled children."[7]

"While some states have a special homeschooling option for parents who are certified teachers, no state requires that every homeschooling parent be a certified teacher.

In fact, research has found little difference between the academic achievement of homeschooled students whose parents were certified teachers and those whose parents were not. They both scored on average much higher than their counterparts in public school."[8]

One of the main reasons that homeschooling is an option for families is due to the tireless work of the Homeschool Legal Defense Association (HSLDA). For 40 years they have fought to keep homeschooling legal and defend parents and children from government overreach. We have been members for about 15 years and I recommend that you look into membership. You can visit them at HSLDA.org to find out more.

Why Should I Homeschool?

Not only can't our kids read, write, or count very well; now they can't drive a nail, plane a board, use a saw, turn a screwdriver, boil an egg, or find ways to amuse themselves and stay healthy. -John Taylor Gatto

In his excellent book *Weapons of Mass Instruction,* John Taylor Gatto states;

"The same young people we confine to classrooms these days once cleared this continent when it was a wilderness, built roads, canals, cities; whipped the greatest military power of earth not once but twice, sold ice to faraway India before refrigeration, and produced so many miracles—from the six-shooter to the steamboat to manned flight—that America spread glimmerings of what open-sourced creativity could do all around the planet...

"Don't let your [children] have their childhoods

extended, not even for a day. If David Farragut could take command of a captured British warship as a preteen, if Ben Franklin could apprentice himself to a printer at the same age…there's no telling what your own kids could do. After a long life, and thirty years in the public school trenches, I've concluded that genius is as common as dirt. We suppress genius because we haven't yet figured out how to manage a population of educated men and women. The solution, I think, is simple and glorious. Let them manage themselves."[9]

In a 2016 survey by the Department of Education "the highest percentage of homeschooled students had parents who said that a concern about the environment of other schools, such as safety, drugs, or negative peer pressure was one reason to homeschool (80 percent). The highest percentage of students' parents reported that among all reasons, a concern about the environment of other schools was the most important reason for homeschooling (34 percent). Seventeen percent of homeschooled students had parents who reported dissatisfaction with academic instruction at other schools as the most important reason for homeschooling, while 16 percent reported a desire to provide religious instruction as the most important reason for homeschooling (table 8)."[10]

One big change in school is that social studies has replaced history. So, your children may not know the same information that you do. They may not come home with a good understanding of George Washington, Abraham

Lincoln, the Pilgrims, or other historical information from around the world.

When new homeschooling families ask about choosing curriculum for their children, the first thing experienced homeschool moms ask is, "How does your child learn?" or "What does your child like to do?" (Video games and playing with friends are not the correct answers.)

You may not know these answers, and that's okay.

We are asking about your child's strengths and weaknesses. To know those, you will need to spend a lot of time with your child in different learning environments. If they were at school eight hours a day, five days a week, that type of observation probably didn't happen.

You saw them in the morning rushing to school. You saw them exhausted at the end of the day. You saw them on the weekends and on school breaks, but you may not have spent the kind of learning time and down time that would allow you to answer those questions. No problem, you'll have time to do that now and finding these answers will be like solving a mystery.

Homeschool students doing traditional homeschooling consistently test one grade or more above their public-school peers. This doesn't mean that will be the result from your first year of homeschool, but those who homeschool over time will.

Should I Have a Schedule or be More Relaxed?

I recommend starting with a schedule. It is so much easier to begin with a schedule and then back off, than to start off easy and try to get your kids to cooperate.

Try to remember when you were in school. Was it easier for the strict teacher to keep students' attention or for the relaxed substitute to keep them on task? You know the answer. If you start your homeschool with structure, you can always make changes later.

I recommend starting your school day at the same time every day. This will stop a lot of whining and complaining once it becomes a habit. Some families start school at 8am, some at 9am and some at 10am. It all depends on you.

What Does a Homeschool Day Look Like?

Laura's Day:

We don't follow a specific schedule in our homeschool, but posted on the refrigerator is a reminder of our goal:

To Have Our Best Day

- Everyone brings their best attitude
- Be dressed and ready by 9 am
- Start the day with breakfast and prayer
- Chores and school before play
- Eat healthy meals at proper times

- Practice piano and violin
- Prep clothes and supplies for the next day
- All dishes done before bed

I've found that the closer we can stick to these simple goals, the more likely we are to have a calm and productive day.

After morning chores my slow-moving-in-the-morning 11th grader usually spends some time practicing piano before heading to her room to work on her lessons. I check in with her from time to time to make sure she's staying on task and not getting too distracted by her phone or whatever art project she's currently working on. She works independently and has due dates for each chapter or unit in her various subjects. When the due date arrives, she has to turn in her work and take the test, ready or not. We used to be more lenient with deadlines but have come to realize the hard deadline is important motivation for completing her work in a timely manner; this stricter system is working better for both of us.

I always remind my 7th grader to do math first while her brain is freshest. Throughout the day, she checks in with me after each subject or anytime she has questions. We do history read alouds and science projects together, but otherwise she works pretty independently. She has a list of subjects to work through each day (not every subject every day), but she doesn't sit still at a desk to work through the list, that's just not how she functions. She can often be found reading her history book in a blanket fort with the guinea pig on her chest or writing an essay on the tree swing while her little sister digs holes nearby.

Play is learning for my preschooler. And no, I don't mean every toy or game is "educational" or every activity is planned with an agenda. Her play is almost completely unstructured. I do set out a few stations at the kitchen table sometimes: a seasonal sensory bin, play dough, letter recognition or counting activities from her school box, peg boards with rubber bands, etc. But that is all completely voluntary. Some days she'll spend a long time working through everything I put out. Other times she'll just do one, request something else, or ignore them altogether. Structured school will come gradually as she becomes developmentally ready for it. Right now, we read lots of books together, run errands and do chores, and play, play, play.

It's important to me that the big girls try to have their lessons wrapped up by the time Dad gets home at 4. The dynamic of our home changes at that point with dinner preparations, everyone wanting to talk to Dad, getting ready for the kids' various evening activities and looking ahead to the next day. If they need additional time for any schoolwork, we usually try to fit that in on Saturday, but even for my high schooler that's the exception, not the norm.

I've also learned we function best if we limit scheduled activities outside the house (during school hours) to one or two days a week. Any more than that and too much of our time at home is taken up with housework, so it's hard to get into a productive rhythm with school. By being careful to limit participation in weekly co-ops, lessons, and park days to something we can manage without pushing our limits, I'm able to leave some flexibility to add in the occasional field trip or errands.

Jessica's Day:

We don't follow a strict schedule, but having a consistent routine or flow is necessary. I notice my kids are more cooperative when they know what to expect from the day. With that in mind, I outline this timeline based on what usually happens, not what I have imposed as the schedule.

This routine has changed over the years based on the number of kids we have, ages, times of extra activities, my own health, my husband's work schedule, etc. We know when it's working and when it's not. When it's not, we change things up. Having this flexibility is one of the most beautiful things about homeschooling!

At 8am I wake the older two kids, the only ones who prefer to sleep in. All the little ones are usually awake by then and eager to start breakfast. This is a firm time, but it is the only thing in the morning that always happens exactly at that time.

Everyone helps prepare breakfast, or watches toddlers or babies while we work. By 8:30, we are usually all sitting down. I might read aloud, or we may listen to a podcast or audiobook during breakfast, but not always.

By around 9:30, breakfast is over. I send everyone to do self-care, and one home care task. Self-care includes brushing teeth, getting dressed if they aren't already, brushing hair, etc. Home care means unloading clean dishes (dirty dishes get done later), clearing and wiping the table, and other tasks that help us move toward starting school for the day—not highly involved tasks.

10am is "table time". Table time work is skill level work like math, handwriting, spelling, and phonics. During table time, I have the older kids take turns rotating on toddler care. I set out an activity, toy, or books for them to engage the 1- and 3-year-old with. It's amazing how well even my 6-year-old can entertain them! I usually give the youngest school-aged child my attention first, since their work gets done the most quickly, then work up to the oldest.

Most of the time our table work is done by lunchtime. The kids take turns making or helping with lunch. Usually, we watch an educational program or go outside for lunch. This is MY break time! I read, eat, or do my housework during this time.

If we don't have any activities for the day, our content work like history, science and social studies gets done in the late afternoon or evening when Dad is home. This is usually in the form of reading, followed by narration or discussion. This happens typically three times per week. Other afternoons we are socializing with friends at the park, at the library, at chess club, or at a sports meet up.

Our morning routine, including table time, is Monday-Friday. Although only the oldest two get table time done on

Thursday when the other kids are getting ready for and attending a daytime gymnastics class. Their school for the day is usually only audiobooks or educational songs in the car. Four days a week still provides the consistency we need to make steady progress on their math and reading skills.

I want to add all of our curriculum is "open and go" meaning I don't have to do much prep before the school day starts. I also don't plan a certain amount of pages or problems each day, but instead track what's done. Some days or weeks a child may move slowly through math but speed through phonics. As long as effort is being made each day, I'm content. In this way a lot of pressure is taken off of them and me, and I'm certain over time they make just as much progress and retain more because I don't push their pace. Another perk of that homeschool flexibility!

My day:

I have a lot to do each day and I also value alone time. My days are structured to give me both time to accomplish everything and time to myself. I get up at 5am and spend the first two hours having a cup of tea, working at my business, exercising, and taking a shower. Our youngest gets up around 7, so that's when the day begins.

At 9am school starts.

We start the day with the most difficult subjects. Our brains are the most alert and able to handle the strain first thing in the school day. We've tried mixing it up, but this has been the best solution for us.

Then it's lunch time.

After lunch time it is recess outside or play time in their room for 1 hour. This gives us some wiggle time before more schoolwork, and it gives me a mental break.

Whenever time is mentioned, set a timer. If you don't, then your kids will come and ask you if the time is up every five minutes, making it a miserable time for both of you. Alternately, one of you will lose track of time. Losing track of time means school doesn't get done until 8 pm and you're both fried. You can avoid these problems by either turning on your phone's timer or getting a cheap kitchen timer that ticks as it moves and makes a loud ding. (A ticking kitchen timer is especially helpful when you first try this as it helps younger kids who need a visual representation of time.)

After the lunch break, it's time for whichever subjects didn't get done before lunch. I'm usually folding laundry, cooking, or cleaning the house. My job is to listen, correct any wrong words, ask and answer questions.

It might look like this:

Billy: In 1892 Colob sailed the ocean

Mom: Columbus

Billy: Columbus sailed the ocean from Spain to…

ANOTHER EXAMPLE IS:

Billy: Ben Franklin said, "Those who would give up essential liberty, to purchase a little temporary safety, deserve neither liberty nor safety."

Mom: That was great reading, now stop for a second. Why do you think Mr. Franklin said that?

If I notice my child is having trouble concentrating during a particular subject, I may ask them to unload the dishwasher or sweep outside for a few minutes to give them an excuse to get up and move, before returning to the subject at hand.

Here is our sample school day:

9:00 math
9:40 history
10:15 language
11:00 lunch
11:45 break time
12:45 art
1:45 science
2:00 school is finished

Vicki Says:

Children are generally *born curious*; they are created to learn. They tend to naturally explore and investigate and learn. But learning and schooling aren't necessarily the same thing.

In the earlier years, even up into primary school, *I won't* usually means *I can't* or *I'm not ready for this yet.* But he doesn't generally know how to process or communicate that, so it sometimes comes out as *I don't want to!* Or even *I'm going to slide from my chair to the floor in a sobbing mess.* (Or maybe that's his mom.)

So, what *is* age- or developmentally appropriate for a younger child? Some children read at age four, while others jump into phonics around age eight—and both can be in the range of normal! Children mature at different rates and focus on different skills at different seasons, and there are a lot of factors to take into consideration.[4] Most children sort of "level out" around third grade, but before that, hold all those scope-and-sequence checklists very loosely, and think of learning as a continuum, not an age-specific menu. They don't need scholastic deadlines. They *do* need lots of outdoor or free play and real-life learning.

OUTDOOR or Free Play

Pediatric occupational therapist Angela Hanscom "discovered that movement through active play, particularly in the outdoors, is absolutely the most beneficial gift we as parents, teachers and caregivers can bestow on our children to ensure healthy bodies, creative minds, academic success, emotional stability, and strong social skills. Children should be getting daily movement experiences throughout the day in order to develop strong and healthy musculoskeletal systems. Musculoskeletal and sensory systems lay the groundwork for higher level mental and physical skills as children age. Ideally, kids of all ages should get at least three hours of free play outdoors a day."[5]

Real-life Learning

If nobody told you that they had to go to school at age 5, what would you be doing with them?[6] What are you doing with them now? Try doing that same thing, but a bit more intentionally. Interact with them naturally—you don't have to invent lots of artificial learning experiences—you have plenty of "real" ones already! (Don't believe me? Check out the articles in the notes at the end of this book, and be sure to read Durenda Wilson's book, *The Unhurried Homeschooler*; it's a quick read–I read it in the hour my banana bread baked!)

So, when your younger student is balking at that new concept you are trying to introduce, first ask yourself if he is *ready* for this new concept; if not, maybe let it go for now and circle back in a few days or weeks. Second, is there a play-based or relevant-in-real-life way to introduce it to him? Or maybe try the strewing method[7] that one mama uses with her four boys: leaving books or activities lying around the house for the kids to find so they think it's *their* idea to try them out!

Chapter 3

Are There Different Ways to Homeschool?

"**Pedagogy** refers to the methods, practices, and purposes of teaching; **curriculum** is what is specifically being taught."
-Pete Hegseth, *Battle for the American Mind*

Pete also wrote that the word **paidagogos** generally means "a leader who walks with students and trains them in manners, academics, and virtue."[11] That's what we are trying to do. You and I are walking with our children through their formative years and training them to have knowledge, character, and manners.

Character training is teaching our children to have "moral excellence and firmness."[12] We teach them what is right and what is wrong in life. For example, it's right to help your neighbor and it's wrong to steal. This must be taught to children and shown by example in everyday life.

As you evaluate each type of homeschool method look for ones that will nurture positive personality traits in each of your children.

Traditional Method

There are several ways that families homeschool. There is the traditional method which I talked about in the beginning, which is educating your children at home with things such as textbooks, workbooks, readers, and a program. This program can be designed either by you or by a curriculum provider and would cover math, history, science, language arts and any electives.

Pros: Ensures you teach all subjects, gives a quality education, rewards children who enjoy seeing how well they are doing, has workbooks for ease of use, identifies a grade level, is great for showing grandparents how well your children are doing in school.

Cons: May be less hands-on, requires reading and writing, is more structured, looks more like regular school.

Charlotte Mason Method

Then there is the Charlotte Mason method, SimplyCharlotteMason.com describes this as, "Charlotte

Mason education is three-pronged: in her words, 'Education is an Atmosphere, a Discipline, a Life.'

Charlotte believed that the ideas that rule your life as the parent make up one-third of your children's education.

By 'Discipline,' Charlotte meant the discipline of good habits—and specifically habits of character.

The other third of education, 'Life,' applies to academics. Charlotte believed that we should give children living thoughts and ideas, not just dry facts."[13]

This is a great approach for some people and can be the perfect fit for both the mom teaching it and the children learning it.

Pros: More relaxed, includes a lot of hands-on and outside activities, uses regular books instead of textbooks or workbooks, doesn't require finding a specific grade level.

Cons: Too relaxed for some families, can lack structure, may not appeal to children who enjoy getting rewards for work well done, may not appeal to parents who want to show work to family members.

Unschooling

The unschooling method is also called "child-led learning". Unschooling doesn't have an actual definition, so I can only tell you from 17 years of homeschool experience what unschooling has looked like to me. Unschooling has its time and place and there are variations of unschooling and traditional schooling that merge, so this is just a general overview so you understand this option and can answer about it intelligently.

Just like there are different types of homeschoolers, there are also different types of unschoolers. Some do a more child-led type of instruction where they allow their children to choose what they are interested in. It can look like anything from allowing your science-minded son to wake up and head outside to study the ecosystem of a stream; or in contrast a parent who only teaches what the child asks to learn.

An unschooling educational environment can work for the family of a child with an especially high IQ. This child is the one who you might find on the living room floor surrounded by books on how to code a robot. If your child wakes up and starts whining about playing video games, this is NOT a viable option.

Some unschooling families call themselves unschoolers, but their houses are full of educational materials, and they still have formal math and language instruction. This might look like each child in a different math textbook, but for the rest of the subjects, they encourage the kids to get books from the library, research on their own and go on field trips to learn.

. . .

Pros: Unschooling allows advanced children to race ahead without the burden of set subjects or particular levels. It is also advantageous for the free-spirited nature lover who never comes inside.

Cons: Parents who don't value education may use the term unschooling to excuse a lack of education for their children or for lazy parenting. This has not been the case with any of the unschooling families I have encountered. However, this is not a good fit for parents who need accountability to make education happen. If your child loves workbook pages and rewards this probably isn't a good choice for them. Children who love to get an A on a test and feel proud of their academic accomplishments, should have that opportunity. (Unschoolers: please leave more information about what unschooling is to you in your review online so we can all learn more!)

Charter Schools

The trend right now is toward charter homeschools. Why? Because they provide money for curriculum and often classes. What that means is that when you enroll your child in the charter, they allot money for you to buy curriculum. Many charters will also pay for classes like gymnastics, karate, or piano.

The money they give you comes from the government. These are public charter schools where you can homeschool your children and do the things you want to do with them while the government pays for it. It is similar to the idea of the money following the child. What that looks like is the charter school will set the standards for what you need to cover and allot you a certain amount of money to cover curriculum and you teach your children. The charter is still required to test your children throughout the year. You may be required to administer the test, (usually online,) or bring your children in for testing because the charter still has to answer for your child's test score.

Part of their process is to send a teacher to meet with you to see specific samples of your child's work. This might be a page of history covering a particular event the charter requires you to teach. This could be a page of math, a page of geography and/or a page of science.

One reason families choose charter schools is because they are scared and would like the guidance and support of someone who can help them through the homeschool process. Unfortunately, numerous families have found that many charter school teachers have no background in homeschooling and are unaware of what curriculum is available or how to organize a homeschool.

As a state organization, they will not pay for religious items. Since the majority of the excellent homeschool curriculum available is Christian based, they will not pay for that. Charter homeschool families still use Christian curriculum. Those families pay for the curriculum themselves and just use the charter funds to purchase supplies, readers, music lessons, tutoring or computer programs. These families turn in a history work sample downloaded online that covers the same topic and have their child do that page and submit it.

Charter schools ask for monthly visits with you and all school employees are mandatory reporters to child protective services of any concerns they may have about your family. They will also require your children to be tested at whatever intervals your school and state require.

Testing doesn't always go well.

During the test week, children often experience crying, breakdowns, eating issues, sleep issues, and anxiety. Kids end up feeling the same pressure they felt during testing in public school. The online test used by California charter schools is particularly stressful for children. If your child gets the problem right, it gives them a harder problem and harder and harder until they get one wrong. For example, if your first grader is completing the math portion and answers 2+2 correctly then the test will ask them a third-grade math problem and if by random chance they answer correctly, then it will ask them a middle school math problem and if they get that one right it will ask them a high school math problem.

This causes the child to look at the screen upset and confused. Then kids break down because every test they have taken in first grade has had first grade problems. And if they know the material, they get each problem right.

This test requires them to get wrong answers on purpose. The kids become scared and confused. They can't pass this test. There is always something they don't know. It has been awful to see parents of charter homeschool programs posting in groups that their kids are crying, breaking down and feeling dumb during the test.

Charter homeschools can also gain access to your home. Some teachers have asked intrusive questions. Sometimes the teachers complain if your child is not at grade level, even if you just pulled them out of public school. This adds a tremendous amount of stress to your first year when you know that whatever your child hasn't been taught was not your fault.

Some of these charter teachers have never taught in a classroom before. Some of them have just graduated from college with a teaching degree. Some of them have been teachers for 20 years and the only experience they have had with homeschooled students are the ones who were forced into public school after they charged their parents with educational neglect. Those teachers are especially hard on homeschool families. Of course, some teachers are excellent educators and advocates. Even better, some are former homeschool parents who, after graduating their kids are now charter schoolteachers.

Keep this in mind if you sign up with a charter school and have a bad experience, you can leave the charter at any time and homeschool independently.

Why One Family Left a Charter School

We decided to join a charter for one year to take advantage of the funding for classes and hands-on activities.

Our family went into it knowing that we would stay with it for one year.

While we enjoyed the money and options that year, the testing caused crying and meltdowns. We also mistakenly attended a school assembly with performers we were not comfortable with.

One reason we didn't stay with the charter was that I didn't want to become accustomed to the government giving me money and asking me to make small compromises, things like:

- Here's $$$, teach these things
- Here's $$$, pick a secular curriculum
- Here's $$$, we will determine if your child is on-track or not
- Here's $$$, attend a school event
- Here's $$$, test your child
- Here's $$$, let us in your house
- Here's $$$, let us talk to your child
- Here's $$$, don't leave

Every family is in a unique position.

What is right for one is not necessarily right for another.

We knew that if we stayed with the charter for longer than one year, we would make allowances for things we didn't agree with.

. . .

PROS: You can get money for books, classes, and activities. If you have foster children or are in a contentious divorce, this is a good option because it is still a public school. If your child has special needs, you can use the charter funds for specialty materials and tutoring.

CONS: Once you get used to getting money from the government for your child's education, it can be very difficult to stop taking it. Charter school employees are mandatory reporters and may report your family for anything they deem harmful. School and state testing are required for each student. You may find yourself put into uncomfortable situations.

Classical Education

Susan Wise Bauer describes the classical education model as, "a three-part process of training the mind. The early years of school are spent in absorbing facts, systematically laying the foundations for advanced study. In the middle grades, students learn to think through arguments. In the high school years, they learn to express themselves. This classical pattern is called the trivium."[14]

There are classical education programs for homeschoolers that meet weekly, such as Classical Conversations. You can also purchase classical education curriculum online through Memoria Press or Classical Academic Press. Other homeschool publishers such as The

Well-Trained Mind are built on the classical education model.

Classical Academic Press explains classical education as the teaching of liberal arts. On their website they ask, "What are the liberal arts? They are grammar, logic, rhetoric (the verbal arts of the trivium), arithmetic, geometry, music, and astronomy (the mathematical arts of the quadrivium). This approach to education also includes the study of Latin. The classical approach teaches students how to learn and how to think."[15]

Pros: There are many positives to pursuing a classical education for your child. Students who have a classical education are generally articulate, knowledgeable about history, and know great works of literature. They can also think critically and understand how to use logic to analyze information.

Cons: Many families find the workload of the classical education model to be overwhelming. The topics introduced in the literature is not always considered age appropriate and introducing mythological gods and goddesses can be confusing to children. Parents for whom English is a second language may find classical education materials too difficult to use.

Pods

Pod schooling is not new, but interest in it has increased dramatically over the past three years. Like unschooling, pods do not have a dictionary definition. When someone talks about starting a homeschool pod, they are usually referring to gathering several families together to pay a teacher to instruct their children several days a week. It is similar to the one-room schoolhouse model.

This has been a good option for families where both parents work and have several friends who want to pod school together. This might look like six seventh-grade students renting a room at a local church to have class together from 9am-3pm Monday through Thursday.

I have watched people attempt to form pods, but the individuality of homeschool families and the need to follow the same curriculum, makes this a hard model to get off the ground.

Pros: This option appeals to parents who need their children to be out of the home for most of the day and want them to be with their peers.

Cons: Pods lack the individualized curriculum that makes homeschool so appealing, it also requires the participants to be around the same age and of similar socio-economic status, to afford the same materials.

What is a Co-op?

Co-ops are cooperative teaching groups for homeschool families. Each one is established by one or two homeschool families who want to get their kids together for certain subjects. Some co-ops are run as formal organizations.

Formal co-ops usually have written agreements that families must sign. These agreements are similar to agreements you might see on a sports team. They go over the structure of the co-op, what the participation rules are, and the code of conduct. There is also a fee each student pays for renting the facility, insurance, supplies, snacks, and any payment given to the parents who teach the classes. Classes at a formal co-op might include language arts, pre-algebra, American history, art, logic, Spanish, or drama. Some formal co-ops are drop-off classes and some require a parent to stay in the building.

These formal co-ops often have credentialed teachers who teach some classes and many require parents to volunteer in a certain number of classes. Classes are normally one to two semesters long.

The type of co-op that is more frequently seen is several homeschool families who decide to get together to cooperatively have classes they enjoy teaching. This might look like six homeschool families meeting at a house or church to have an art class and science class once a week. The parents either take turns teaching or helping in the class. There is usually a small fee to cover supplies. After class there is a group lunch picnic.

These informal co-ops give kids a chance to learn from someone who is passionate about a particular subject and attending helps facilitate friendships for the kids and the parents. We have enjoyed being part of both types of co-ops.

Not every homeschool family or class is a safe place to drop your kids. The first time you bring your kids somewhere, sit in the class or just outside the door so you can hear what's going on inside. Let people and organizations earn your trust. However tempted you may be, don't just drop and run. Get recommendations from other homeschool moms you trust and take time to get to know people and make good decisions for your kids.

If there is a subject I'm lazy about doing or if it's a particularly hard time such as a new baby or a move, then I enroll my children in a formal co-op class or buy a video program for that subject. That way I can ensure my children will learn that subject.

Chapter 4

I Think I'm in, Now What?

Hooray! Welcome to the club. We're so glad you're here!

How do I Pick Curriculum?

Let me ask you some questions about your fears, hopes and goals.

1. What are your worries as you begin homeschooling?

Do you worry that you won't do a good enough job? That your children may not get the best education? That your mother-in-law thinks your children will be uneducated? Or that your ex-husband doesn't think homeschoolers are properly socialized? These answers change what I would recommend. In those cases, I recommend a more structured homeschool curriculum such as Abeka for your first year. This is so you can get used to how homeschool works, get a lot of guidance through their comprehensive teacher's guides and stay on-track with a tried-and-true curriculum that exceeds state standards. Other curriculum such as Bob Jones (BJU) and Alpha Omega (AOP) are also good choices but I prefer Abeka's presentation of the materials. In my opinion, Abeka is more engaging and less textbook-ish.

2. What are your goals for your homeschool and for your children?

IF YOUR FIRST *goal is to detox them from a stressful school environment and Zoom school meltdowns, then a more relaxed, family-centered approach may meet your needs for this year. Two curriculum providers that offer that type of product are Sonlight or My Father's World.*

3. How old are your children?

DO *you have a very advanced 3-year-old who needs to be challenged? Then maybe a more traditional approach would be appropriate. Do you have a 7-year-old with ADHD? Then a more physically demanding, hands-on approach would be the answer. Do you have a middle school or high school-aged child? Then maybe a more independent curriculum would work. There are some curriculum providers that I love but wouldn't recommend for high school. There are others I love for high school, but I don't like their elementary grade materials. You will need to spend some time looking over different curriculum to find what stands out to you. This includes looking inside the books to see how the information is presented and reading reviews. You will know when it's the right one when you love the curriculum too!*

4. What is your home and work life like?

IF YOU CONTINUE *to work while homeschooling, that changes the curriculum you choose. Do you have six kids and a newborn? Then a curriculum with subjects that can be taught together for all ages, with independent math books, might be a good choice. (See Jessica's school day.)*

FOR YOUR FIRST YEAR, I would tell you that the curriculum you choose should be easy for you to implement, since you are learning more about homeschooling and investigating how your children learn.

There are three things you need: the best method for picking curriculum, to know what courses are available, and to be encouraged. You can learn these three by visiting the websites of the curriculum mentioned below and ordering their free catalogs. These catalogs are unlike normal catalogs. Each of them contains articles, helpful information, stories from homeschool families and of course, information about each book. I order these and keep them in places where I'll look at them throughout the year.

1. Sonlight
2. Abeka
3. Christian Book Distributor's homeschool catalog

Many people think that the "complete curriculum" books you find at Costco, Walmart or in bookstores are curriculum. They are not. The word curriculum refers to the lessons and the content that is taught in a particular course or program.

Curriculum is very subjective. Pick one that you love and that your kids enjoy.

It doesn't matter if it's the best math program out there. If you hate it and dread the very thought of pulling it out each day, then it's not the right one for your family.

If you're excited because you found one that you understand and can't wait to use it with your kids, then your enthusiasm will be contagious!

If your kids hate it and every day crying begins as soon as you pull it out, then it may not be the right one.

However, if your child hates everything and cries about

all of it, that's a character training problem, not a curriculum problem.

Remember to reward the things your children are doing right, but don't reward things they are doing wrong. If a child is mistreating you or refusing to complete their schoolwork, don't reward that behavior with time off. Make sure you have a consequence.

Character Training

1. Respect the authority of your parents
2. Pay attention
3. Obey willingly & immediately
4. Learn rules and apply them
5. Do your best
6. Learn to love hard work
7. Finish the job
8. Do the right thing, because it is the right thing
9. Work hard
10. Love wisdom
11. Choose things that are excellent
12. Develop the habits of orderliness, carefulness, alertness, persistence, honesty, accomplishment, cooperation, faithfulness, accuracy, perseverance, self-control, attentiveness, fairness, thoroughness, confidence, responsibility, decisiveness, effort, steadfastness, discipline, endurance, helpfulness, reasonableness, neatness, patience, good judgment, and loyalty

If you're unhappy with the curriculum you have, see if you can tweak it to make it work for you.

If your workbook is black and white, take an evening and add stickers and highlights to the page to brighten it up. If it's not going deep enough, find some manipulatives to add and some videos to go deeper. If it's got too much repetition, go through it and cross out sections your child already knows and doesn't need any practice on.

I recommend finishing what you start. You are training your children. If they see you quit things, they will learn to do the same. There are exceptions but see what you can do to finish the curriculum this year and if necessary, make different choices next year.

You may also hear the term "eclectic homeschooling" which means that you don't use one curriculum for all your subjects, you use different methods for each subject.

If you've just started homeschooling, you may not have noticed that there are some subjects that your child does well at and others where they struggle. Each year our family has a focus. If your child struggles in language arts (grammar, writing, reading,) then you can focus this coming year on language arts and get a language program that is deep.

If you do this, you might choose to go light with science and history by just reading through the books together. That way you have more time and energy to devote to language arts.

The next year you can choose to focus on science and

get a program that has a lot of science experiments. This is just something that has worked well for us. Balance comes over time, from adding all the years together. When I make mistakes in one direction, I can make corrections and go in the opposite direction the following year.

Going 110% on each subject can lead to lots of frustration for you and the kids.

Each year, we have one or two subjects we focus on.

Here are some examples of this for early elementary.

Kindergarten's focus would be on language and math. We would still do science and history, but they would just be something I read to that child on the couch, no workbook or testing.

First grade's focus would continue to be language and math and if I noticed that my child was having trouble with reading or math, I would take more time with one of those. We would continue to read through history and science together.

Second grade's focus again continues to be language and math, but science would have some more hands-on time with experiments like making slime or oobleck, field trips to the zoo or walks in nature observing what we were learning about in our textbook. Taking a magnifying glass into the yard, making pipe cleaner models of the inside of flowers. History might include longer discussions about our history textbook, field trips to museums and watching the *Liberty's Kids* series.

Third grade will look a lot like second grade except that

the books will be longer, the words more complex and the concepts will take longer to teach and understand.

I suggest getting a pre-packaged language curriculum with a teacher's guide for your first year or two. After that you can decide if you want to create your own.

Workbooks are good for reinforcing what kids have been taught. They are for practicing and reviewing topics. Workbooks are not *for* teaching kids. Don't just buy a workbook for math. Kids need a full math program for instruction. Unless you enjoy teaching math and sitting next to your children as they work on math, I would recommend getting video instruction for mathematics. Good choices for this are Math-U-See, Dive into Math, Abeka Academy and Teaching Textbooks.

Find somewhere to be alone for an hour with a pen and paper. Think about each of your children:

1. How does that child learn best? (Is it by reading, hands-on activities, listening to audiobooks, through songs, in group classes, by watching a video?)
2. Thinking back on the past year, how has that child understood each subject? (Really grasped it, had difficulty with it, excelled at it, loved it, hated it, seems a year behind, needs a refresher, didn't grasp basic parts of it, could use the same level or grade but by a different curriculum to reinforce the concepts, needs someone who loves it as much as they do to teach it.)

3. What worked and what didn't work?
4. Which curriculum/program/method did I like or dislike? Why?
5. What does my child need? (A curriculum with songs on cd or a video or something interactive or a particular subject taught by someone else? Would they like more quizzes because they love to test themselves or would they like a class with peers because they love to work as a group?)
6. What does this child need to learn to be a successful, independent, adult?
7. I may not enjoy teaching (name a subject) _____ but it's important for my child's future that they be able to

    _____

    (communicate effectively, write complete sentences, understand the natural world, have a good grasp of history, think critically, logically decipher information for truth and accuracy, be mathematically competent so they aren't cheated at the store/on taxes/during employment.) Without this skill, my child will be at a disadvantage in the world as an adult.
8. Looking at #2, which subjects do I need to incorporate into school to accomplish that goal?
9. How do I need to break up that information to get it completed by the time my child graduates from high school? *Are you putting off teaching English until the 12th grade? If so, can they*

> *learn all of that and really understand it in one year or would it be better to introduce it slowly, over time, so they can absorb it and make it part of how they write naturally? Can health be skipped as a "subject" each year and just be taught officially at 8th grade to cover anything you've missed in normal conversation over the years?*
> 10. Which curriculum/program/book/methods do I think will work best to accomplish each subject I want to teach this year?

This is the process I go through each year as I choose curriculum for my children.

You need to know *why* you chose your curriculum and what your goals are for each child.

> *"You can't hit a target you aren't aiming for."*
> -Zig Ziglar

Are Homeschool Kids in the Same Grade Level as Public School?

Many parents find that kids brought home from public school were not taught the basics. You may find that taking your sixth grader out of public school and putting her into a sixth grade homeschool curriculum may not work. She may not have the foundation required for understanding 6th grade homeschool curriculum. Another thing you may encounter is that she may have been doing pre-algebra in school (pre-algebra generally means a review of everything prior to algebra and introduces some algebra terms) so looking at sixth grade homeschool math that isn't pre-algebra may make you think, she's farther ahead than homeschool kids. But as you continue through the school year, you may notice that she's struggling with even the simplest of concepts. Yes, the school said she was at a certain math level, but she may have been rushed through it and never really understood it.

In homeschool we teach for mastery. If our kids don't get a concept, we stop and find another way to explain it. We search YouTube or we might realize that our child isn't mature enough to grasp that concept. In that case, we can stop and decide how to proceed. An example of this might be a child having difficulty with long division.

As you work with your child, you realize he doesn't understand how division works, but more than that, he doesn't understand how multiplication works.

Now you must decide what to do.

Do you keep moving forward, knowing that what you're saying sounds like Charlie Brown's teacher? Or do you:

- Take a break from math for a day or two to see if he gets it in a few days?
- Stop and go backward, choosing to print out some multiplication worksheets and do those for several days?
- Spend a week listening to multiplication songs

and doing multiplication problems until multiplication comes naturally?
- Print out some super simple division problems?

After that, you could return to the original math lesson with this new knowledge and confidence.

This is homeschooling.

One of the cool things I learned a long time ago is that 8th grade is a review year. Kids basically review everything they've learned in K-7th grade, to prepare for high school. Knowing this gives you options. You could skip 8th grade. You could focus on the subjects that your child struggles with and do the other subjects half-heartedly. You could investigate an apprenticeship for your child that year. Your options are limitless!

Should I Buy New or Used Books?

Whether you use new or used curriculum is completely up to you. Here are some guidelines to help you decide which to purchase. If you're only reading through a subject, then used books are great. An example of this is that you're going to focus on language arts this year, that's your main priority. You also want to cover history, but not as in-depth as language arts. Maybe you'll read history on the couch with all your children. History would then be the perfect subject to buy used. Why? Because you can pay pennies for items you just want to read through once. You don't care if another family highlighted parts of the book or answered the chapter questions in pencil and then erased them. You're just going through the subject to give your kids a general overview of it. If you're doing this, I recommend Abeka's history books for grades pre-K through 4th grade. The stories in them will engage all ages, including adults.

If you'd like to save on something, the subjects you are just reading through are the perfect places to do that.

What can you find used?

There are people who begin to homeschool and then change their mind after two weeks or order curriculum and then hear about a local class and use that instead. These people will often have their books, tests, quizzes, and teacher's guides for sale as complete, unused sets on eBay. Other families know they are homeschooling for the long haul and have their kids take care of their books and write answers down in notebooks instead of in the workbook or book. Then they sell the like-new set on eBay for a little extra money.

If you're buying a used teacher's guide or answer key, verify the exact edition number on all the books. For example, if you buy the *Saxon 6/5 Second Edition* math book, the only answer key that will go with the correct lessons and problems is the *Saxon 6/5 Second Edition Answer Key*. The Saxon 6/5 first edition or third edition will almost never line up with the other editions. This is very important to know and verify before purchasing the student book and the teacher book separately. For first editions there isn't always something that names them as first editions on the front of the book or on the copyright page, but you can go to the copyright page and look at the year the book was published and verify they were published in the same year. Occasionally you may find a curriculum where the second edition book only has very minor changes, like pictures updated or pages laid out better, but usually the book and answer keys are not compatible.

When you buy something that doesn't need an answer key, like readers, then buying used is a great option! If you buy really used or really old books, this can save you hundreds of dollars. For example, if a science book costs $29 new, but you can find the 1980s version of the book on eBay for $1.25 and you buy one for each grade level of your seven children, you would save $194.25. When I bought elementary health books for my kids, I didn't care if the books were the 1980s versions. Why? Because eating healthy meals, getting exercise, and getting enough rest would not change from year to year. I didn't care if the pictures in the book were old. I also wasn't worried about which grade they were written for. If I liked the material in the book, I bought it. A sixth grader can read a 4th grade health book. A 3rd grader can read a 2nd grade health book. Since I teach my children about being healthy each day, this isn't a subject I wanted to cover every school year.

You can find these older editions on eBay, on used homeschool book websites, at used book sales, at library book sales, at garage sales, in thrift stores, for free in giveaway piles, on Craigslist or on Facebook marketplace. This way you can spend your homeschool budget for fun things like field trips or classes.

"Readers" are especially great to buy used or old. The term "readers" means the non-textbooks your kids are supposed to read. Older kids would just read these to themselves. In the elementary grades, they would read them aloud to you. There are often questions at the end of the chapters (as there are in history and science books) but those are designed to be used in a classroom. The teacher needs to verify that the students have read the material and have understood what they read. You already know that your children have read the chapter, so you don't need these questions. I usually just ask my children to tell me about what they've read.

"Mom, I read chapter one."

"Great! What was it about?"

"Well, there was this dog and he got lost so the people were trying to find him, but..."

For history or science, you can have them read the comprehension questions aloud to you while you're doing the dishes and tell you the answers.

"Question one is who is Genghis Khan?"

"Great, who was he?"

"He led the Mongol Empire."

"Terrific."

"Question two is where was the Mongol Empire located? I don't know."

Tell them to look back on what they've read and find it, then tell you the answer. It's not something you need to grade or stress over, it's just a review of the material they've covered. What's important is that they covered the material and that they understood it.

You can also do what some families do and not write in your books and turn around and sell them when you're done.

Textbooks are just convenient groupings of things people think each grade should know. They are there for ease of use, they aren't the end-all-be-all.

I like to vary the subjects that we use textbooks with each year.

Some years we need textbooks or workbooks for subjects I want my children to learn, but I don't have any passion for. Some years are just survival years (a new baby, health issues, etc.) Some years we are hitting one or two subjects hard and I just want a textbook for another subject that we will read and not delve into.

But the beauty of learning is to be immersed in a subject and see how it relates to real life.

A great way to introduce the study of history is to pick one point in time to concentrate on. To accomplish this, I chose a video game I grew up with, *The Oregon Trail*. It's available now as a retro handheld game. The object of *The Oregon Trail* is to make it from Independence, Missouri, to Oregon City, Oregon. To play the game, you have to budget your money, buy enough supplies to survive, hunt for food and barter with people along the way. Your kids think it's just a game, but they will learn history, use math skills and become familiar with United States geography.

Using this game allows you to pinpoint a particular point in "the olden days" and when you learn about the Pilgrims, you can say, "The Pilgrims were before the Oregon Trail." When you learn about the civil rights movement, you can say, "This was after the Oregon Trail." Having a specific point in time gives your kids a solid frame of reference. They could even make a timeline to help illustrate this.

If you visit a museum, you will see things that relate to the Oregon Trail time period and you can explain that to your children. Get books at the library about the Oregon Trail. Make time to watch documentaries about the Oregon Trail and check out books about the famous trail guides and landmarks along the way.

A similar retro handheld game is *Where in the World is Carmen Sandiego*. This game takes children around the globe as they try to find stolen artifacts. I have fond memories of my siblings and I gathered around our Commodore 64 computer with notebooks and encyclopedias and an atlas as we tried to figure out the clues.

Which Things Make Homeschooling Easier?

1. Make freezer meals or buy frozen meals for your first week of school. Inevitably, your husband will walk in the door, and you'll be shocked that the whole day has passed and you haven't even thought of dinner. That's because

for the first week we're not sure how long each subject is going to take and don't have a real schedule yet.

2. Prioritize social events like weekly park days. Social events will be the first things that you'll want to let go of when you're feeling overwhelmed or behind. But they are the best for giving all of you a refreshing break and for helping you cope.
3. Start strong! A lot of families like to ease into the subjects. For our family that was counterproductive. The first few months of school have always been our most productive. Those are the days when we are the most excited. We have new books, new classes, new smells, new pencils, and new enthusiasm for school. We jump in with both feet and do every subject, knowing that by the end of the school year I'll be yelling, "Just do math and language, and call it a day!"
4. Warn your husband that the first week is going to be hard and that you'll need his patience when nothing else gets done. No laundry, dishes or yard work will get done on time.
5. After your first week, give yourself a little reward, like going for a walk with a friend, reading a good book or some time alone.
6. Do your own version of meal prep or cook 3-4 pounds of ground beef over the weekend, then

divide it up into zip top freezer bags and stick them in the freezer. If you find out it's dinnertime and you didn't plan anything you can grab one of these frozen ground beef bags and throw it into spaghetti sauce, microwave it for tacos, make hamburger macaroni and cheese, have beef stew, put it in ramen noodles with some frozen veggies, or have quick nachos. You can also make hamburger patties ahead of time and freeze them along with hamburger buns for quick meals. Try cutting up fruits and vegetables over the weekend for salads, snacks, and quick stews. You can also find crock pot meals to start in the morning before school and overnight oatmeal recipes for breakfasts.
7. Make a school supply shopping list at the beginning of each school year and load up on the supplies you and the kids need at the cheapest prices they will be all year. Even if they don't really need anything, it will help them get excited about the new school year.

I don't want to teach my children that they get a prize for everything they do in life, however it is nice for them to have a little happy moment for schoolwork that is well done.

The system that has worked for us is:

- On tests, get an A, visit the prize box
- On tests, get a B, earn a scratch-n-sniff sticker

- On daily work, get an A, earn a sticker

My kids *love* taking tests so they can visit the prize box. Our prize box has inexpensive things like fancy pens, fun erasers, dollar store items, treats, and sometimes a higher-priced item like a book.

Are There any Curriculums You Recommend?

Yes. I prefer to use a curriculum that has been around for a while and has shown excellent results. These are a few I can recommend, but Mary Pride's website and books will give you many more options. I have a link to her website at NinaHelpsYouHomeschool.com.

There is a quick way to get started with very little stress or shopping around. It will give you time to learn more about homeschooling and explore your options while your child is still learning, it is to start with Abeka Academy's unaccredited independent study.

Abeka is quite rigorous and as you'll see in the sample consult at the end of the book, there are particular ways I recommend using it. It is also one of the curriculum providers that I would not necessarily recommend in its entirety for older grades. When you buy it for preschool through third grade, the workload is manageable. This allows your children to still have plenty of outdoor time. However, the workload takes longer and becomes more difficult as the grades go up. This is perfect for families who prefer a rigorous educational program for their children.

Those who would like more time in junior high or high school for out of the home activities can easily continue with Abeka Academy by simply choosing their individual subject option or purchasing the entire year but only doing certain subjects.

The Abeka Academy teachers are extremely skilled at video instruction and since Abeka has been used by homeschooling families and elite Christian schools for so long, their methods are excellent. In the video instruction, the teacher will ask questions of the class and then turn to the camera and say, "Now students watching, you answer this question." Then they pause for an answer and have one student in the classroom answer.

The beauty of using this program your first year is that you will learn how to schedule and teach your children with plenty of help and modeling. You'll hear and see how Abeka uses its materials and how they structure the school day. Then the next year you can buy just the student and teacher books from Abeka and teach your children yourself. In your third homeschool year, you can pick from a variety of curriculums. By then you will have a better understanding of how each of your children learns and where they excel or struggle. Abeka academy also comes with your daily lesson plan to tell you exactly what your child is going to do that day.

. . .

THEIR VIDEO OPTION is also great for:

- Teaching a subject that you don't want to teach
- An older child to do one or two subjects alone, as you teach younger children
- Help when you can't teach or if you work during the day

For math your first year, Teaching Textbooks is a good option. This is a math program that teaches and grades everything for you. This happens automatically and is online. They also make a paper version.

We used this for a year and a half with my youngest, while we were focusing on other subjects.

It was great the first year we used it. By the middle of the second year, it wasn't working anymore. The concepts were too abstract to sink in through online learning. When you type something into a computer, it's not the same thing as writing it down with pen and paper. There are different neural pathways in the brain that are formed when you write something down.

If your child is a wiz at math, then he or she could use Teaching Textbooks and just move forward at a faster pace or start in a grade above. It was a great fit for us the first year we used it, but not the second, so your results may vary. I like it for first year homeschoolers because it will ease you into the homeschool routine and help you see where your child is in math.

For those who feel like they learned nothing in school or

that they don't see the importance of teaching language arts, remember that we have already had this teaching. We can talk about the necessity of teaching these subjects because we have already learned how to read and write. Failing to teach our children the fundamentals is failing to teach them the very things that will help them excel. They may choose not to further their education. They may choose to work for themselves, in this case understanding math and how to communicate will be essential. They may choose to be garbage handlers or groundskeepers, but if you don't provide them with the skills to add up their paychecks or write a proper email to a customer, then you're setting them up for failure.

We're doing a disservice to our kids if we allow them to fail so early.

Some of the best homeschool resources will seem old-fashioned or uncool at first. They may turn you off, but over time they will become heartwarming favorites with familiar faces. As you research curriculum watch out for woke values in non-religious school curriculum.

You've heard me mention several of the curriculum options below. These are ones I think are worth researching to see if they are a good fit for you. There is additional information at NinaHelpsYouHomeschool.com. There are also many review videos on YouTube. Just type in the curriculum's name and the word "review" for example, "Teaching Textbooks review."

- Apologia

- Master Books
- Drive Thru Menu Math
- Alpha Omega (AOP)
- The Critical Thinking Company
- Saxon Math (preferably 1st and 2nd editions, but new editions are fine)
- Story of the World (books, audiobooks, and activity books)
- Handwriting Without Tears (HWT)
- Times Tales
- Challenge Math by Edward Zaccaro
- Common Sense Science
- Learning Language Arts Through Literature (LLATL)
- Mystery of History (MOH)
- Institute for Excellence in Writing (IEW)
- Math-u-See (MUS)
- Sonlight

Vicki Says:

Does your student know what the agenda is for the day, and what "finished for today" looks like? Would you be motivated to work diligently if it felt as though every time you finished something, someone just gave you another assignment? There's not much incentive to get finished, is there? Our kids' days can feel daunting—or even unending.

So, it was important to me that my kids see the lesson plan, that they know what the expectation was for the day, to help me evaluate if it was reasonable, and that there was an ending point each day for my demands on their attention.

While I was writing this (on a deadline, of course), I time-chunked some blocks of time to hunker down and hammer it out. This is how my "sit down and work on your assignment" time worked out.

- I did two loads of laundry.
- I updated the photo gallery on my website.
- I made a batch of cookies.
- I checked work e-mails.
- I made travel arrangements for an upcoming speaking engagement.

If there were a tactful way to put a "shaking my head" emoji into a book, this is where it would go!

Maybe it was my highly distractible brain kicking in, or maybe it was just too much to handle in one (or five) sittings, and I needed to break it up, accomplish some other tasks that were on my mind, or let my brain process in between paragraphs.

It's possible that this is how our kids are as soon as we ask them to sit still and work on something for what feels like ages to them. Our kids are people. And sometimes that dawdling kiddo isn't being rebellious or lazy or slow. Sometimes he's just distracted, or he's on overload and needs a brain break.

Remember the old adage *you can lead a horse to water but you can't make him drink?* That may be so, but I propose that the corollary to that statement is: *But you sure can salt his oats!*

So... I *"salted my own oats"* with the knowledge that I'd feel good when I'd gotten my thoughts organized on paper. I made sure it was a task that I was *mature enough in my abilities* to handle. I gave myself *choices* in how and when I wrote. I internalized a *plan and expectations*. I made it *relevant* to my passion for encouraging homeschoolers. And I drew on my *connection* to Nina—my friend—and thus aspired to honor and respect her by getting this to her in a timely manner.

And the now-thirsty proverbial horse drank the water.

How Much Does it Cost to Homeschool?

Don't let money get in the way of a great bonding and educational experience for you and your kids. There are free homeschool programs such as AmblesideOnline, Easy Peasy All-in-One Homeschool, and The Good and the Beautiful. I have not used any of these so I cannot speak about them knowledgably.

Without using a free curriculum, for early elementary you can easily homeschool for $150 a year per child. If you buy used or use library books and visit thrift stores, you could do it for even less. There is no rule that you need to spend up to $1,500 a year for a full book and instruction video package.

I think the difference in curriculum costs is also centered on the questions parents ask. If the question is, "What am I required to teach for first grade?" Then a cheaper curriculum is an option. If the question is, "What information does my child need to know?" Then a more comprehensive curriculum is a better choice.

The first question is about the parent. The second question is about the child.

When you are just starting out, you don't even know where to begin and what questions to ask. As you saw in chapter one, I didn't ask either of these. I was too clueless to even know they were questions. But as you check out programs and have conversations about cost, these are important questions.

If you're talking with your spouse and the question is, "How much is this going to cost us?" Then knowing what your goals are is very important.

All families make tremendous sacrifices in order to homeschool their children. Families for whom money is tight are choosing their children's future over making more money for the household. I admire and respect these families for the strength they show. Their children have a chance at a better future with a far better education than the public school can provide.

Middle-income families have the option to look at more expensive curriculum and use the payment plan options that most of them provide. The education they are providing is equivalent to a private school education for a fraction of the cost.

Going back to the question of, "How much is this going to cost us?" There is another question, "What will it cost us to send them to public school?" You are saving money by not buying school clothes, backpacks, classroom snacks, and endless supplies of tissues for the classroom. There is also a cost to their mental wellbeing, such as being exposed to drugs, things happening in the bathroom, things happening in the locker room, that creepy teacher, what's in those books and the ugly peer pressure. Instead of past generations who said, "what doesn't kill you makes you stronger," we have a generation of kids who are terrified of everything.

One thing that I've both loved and hated is that the voice in my children's head is my own. I hate it when they repeat something dumb I've said. I love it when they fall down in life and instead of hearing the voice of taunting classmates they hear, "You can do this. Try again."

Higher income families make the sacrifice in perception. You may feel that your peers look down on your choice, but who said that sending your children to private school was the best option? The same issues in public school happen in the private schools. There is also the added strain of families whose children they have kicked out of public schools. These families pay to have the school keep their out-of-control child in school at the expense of the teacher's ability to teach and the other children's safety and ability to learn.

While no method of schooling has a 100% success rate, you can guarantee your child will not be harmed at school, if they aren't at school.

Chapter 5

Should my House Look Like a School?

How do I Create a "Learning Environment"?

While trying to counter the forced government schooling, also known as public school, some homeschoolers tell new families not to "school at home." What they are saying is don't attempt to model a typical school day at home. But what it can sound like to new homeschooling parents is, "Don't do anything the school does."

Often new homeschoolers create a schoolroom in their house with desks, a flag and a chalkboard or whiteboard. They use their memories from elementary school classrooms to create a fun learning environment for their children.

While this is a fun and creative idea, it's unnecessary

and many long-term homeschooling parents don't find this situation sustainable. Why? Because five hours into your hardest homeschool day, you still won't be able to leave the schoolroom to cook dinner or do a load of laundry.

Most of us "do school" all around the house. It's great to have a desk, crates or storage closet to keep all their school stuff in, but having a set area for school isn't usually necessary.

Families work together at the kitchen table or on the couch or on the floor. We just need a place to hold books, workbooks and supplies.

We've had desks for each of our kids, we've had a group table, we've had bins, now that I only have one child left at home, we use two crates to hold all our school materials for the year.

Make learning zones in your house, like workstations. One zone is the computer, facing the rest of the house, so you can watch what your children are doing on the computer at all times. Send your children to the couch or on the living room carpet or to lie down with the dog and curl up with a blanket while they read their history textbook or daily reading books. Use the kitchen bar area for art or reading their science book to you as you cook dinner. Send them to lie on their bed while they draw for art class. Use the kitchen table for math. It's not unusual to see kids reading upside down in their tree fort or coloring their anatomy workbook outside in the grass.

Kids with more sensory needs will enjoy reading while on a swing or shouting math facts while jumping on a mini trampoline.

Some days, I cut up all the math problems and hide them around the house. The kids have to find each problem, complete it and find the next one.

Never put computers in your kids' rooms. Never. No exceptions. I recently saw an ad for a parental control filter that said, "Stop p*rn other filters miss." Did you catch that? They claim their filter will stop things that the other filters were created to stop and yet still allow to get through to your kids. Filters miss things all the time and the p*rn industry makes its money by making people addicted to their product and bypassing the filters to get more customers. It makes them money. Your child is a consumer, and all manufacturers want people to be addicted to their products, so does this industry. No matter how responsible or trustworthy your child is, he or she is still a vulnerable child. Adults can't stay away from these things, so don't think your pliable child with a growing brain will withstand them. The same thing applies to phones and tablets.

If your child needs a phone, there are options such as Gabb Wireless and Wisephone that do not have internet access. Kids can use them for calling and texting, but they have no apps or internet capability.

Part of creating a learning environment may be to remove electronics until after 4pm or only on the weekends. It may also include removing streaming services or apps like Disney+.

As you reevaluate what your life and family look like, pay attention to the shows your kids watch. I think you'll see what we did, that most shows are about kids who are smarter than their parents, lying to their parents, sneaking out, having attitudes, smart remarks, and the adults are portrayed as dumb or unworthy of respect or obedience.

Many parents have become so angry at the programming that is pumped into our children's minds that they have started watching old shows like *Leave it to Beaver, Father Knows Best, The Adams Family, Ozzie and Harriet, The Dick Van Dyke Show, The Waltons* and *Little House on the Prairie*. The TikTok effect is real. You'll see its effect if your children have a hard time sitting still to watch one of these episodes. You will have to help them concentrate for longer periods of time and learn to focus on things.

Just from observing teens and young adults around you, you can see that apps like TikTok and watching YouTube shorts trains the brain to have a shorter attention span. As parents, we must do the opposite and help our kids have a longer attention span. Watch *The Social Dilemma* to get the full picture of what is happening to our brains.

A big change between our generation of parents and the generations before us is that we often feel that we have to explain things to our kids. When I'm cooking three foods on the stove and listening to the dog bark at the neighbor and my child asks me for something, saying no isn't hard. When that child asks, "Why not?" is when it gets sticky. I have 90% of my attention on other things and using that 10% to come up with an acceptable answer is actually quite hard on my brain. The bottom line is, "because I said so."

That seems to be an unacceptable answer right now. Parents think we need to sit down and explain to our two-year-old why they can't have gummy bears for breakfast. There are so many things about this that we need to think about. Is it reasonable for a child to question a parent like this? Would I want my four-year-old to question me when he's running into the street, and I scream for him to stop? Is my 15-year-old asking me why because he genuinely wants to understand the psychological damage caused by too much time on electronics?

We all know that the answer to these questions is "no." They are questioning us or asking why because they want what they want. It's time to free ourselves from the need to answer every question our children ask. Sometimes the answer is, "just because." Give yourself that freedom.

I think you'll find that going with your gut is almost always the right answer. "Can I go play at the new neighbor's house?" When you look over to see the uncle who lives with them, you get a creepy feeling.

You have no obligation to think of a reason to say no to this. It's okay to just say no. Sometimes we can't put our finger on why we are uncomfortable with something or why we feel like no is the right answer, but the longer I live, the more I'm relieved that I went with my gut on things.

A body language expert would probably tell you that dozens of processes were happening when you made each decision. That your brain caught things you weren't even aware of in the other person and put all of those together to give you a warning.

The opposite can be true as well. You may not be able to explain why you're sure something is the right answer. Maybe that's your answer to why you decided to homeschool. "Why are we homeschooling? Because we felt like it was the right thing to do."

Just like you don't have to answer to your child when they are being demanding, you also don't have to answer to other people. The person scanning your groceries doesn't need to know why your kids are not in school. It's easy to get caught off guard and stumble for an answer, but it's freeing to know that you don't have to give one.

As you feel more empowered in your role as a homeschool parent, you will see educational opportunities everywhere. One year we heard about the movie *Sergeant York*, a terrific movie that is a true story. Since the movie takes place during World War I, my son and I started learning about World War I. We visited museums and veteran centers. He dug a trench in the backyard and had fake battles with his friends. They watched the movie together. We took out maps and found the places where the battles took place, and we bought the World War I Map Game by Learningames and played it until we had all the places memorized. Thinking back on that year is a fun memory, and it was a great year of learning for us both.

For some subjects, like geography, you can use a game instead of a textbook. Instead of flash cards or drills, math games and history games are great reinforcement for what your kids have just learned.

In *The Read-Aloud Handbook*, author Jim Trelease recommends allowing kids to read below their reading level when they are reading for pleasure. He says the ease of reading below their reading level can cultivate a love of reading in children who don't always enjoy it.

I got sneaky with this and put lower-level reading books in places where my kids would be bored like in the car, in the bathroom or at the kitchen table. If I place a book in these places and don't mention it, they will usually pick it up and start reading it on their own.

This won't work, however, if your child has entertainment at their fingertips with a phone, tablet, video game or computer. Kids need to be bored in order to start thinking outside the box. They need to lie on the grass and look up at cloud shapes with friends and dig in the dirt looking for worms. They need to stare at the wall and make shapes or faces out of textured walls. This is how we got our great music, from bored people hearing songs in their heads.

I'm sure we've all seen the meme asking how many talented musicians, artists, inventors, and scientists have never existed because kids were never bored long enough to create.

We don't want to deprive our children of being bored. It's in our boredom that ideas for books and inventions come.

The other day, a mom asked our Facebook group how we get everything accomplished. The answer is, we don't. One day, the house is clean, but we only got through half our subjects. The next day, the school day is fantastic, but the house looks like it was robbed. Something has to give. You are rarely going to have everything go perfectly.

Years ago, I learned to put the house back together 30 minutes before my husband came home from work. Trying to clean throughout the day just left me exhausted, and the house was a mess by the time he came home.

If I have dinner ready and the house is in good shape after a day of school, I feel like I'm queen of the world. The tips I gave you in chapter 4 will help. If you picture yourself as a juggler with ten balls in the air, imagine that every day at least one ball is going to drop. The nice thing is that once you get a good rhythm, you'll drop fewer balls each day. Keep picking them up and starting again.

Are There Community Resources for Homeschoolers?

It may take several months to find the resources in your community, but most cities have group classes for homeschoolers. An example of this might be an art class put on by your local art or pottery studio. Your local makers' club might have a robotics class for homeschoolers. Churches may have their classrooms rented out for homeschool classes or co-ops. Piano teachers often have homeschool group classes or lessons during the day. Stables offer homeschool riding lessons and classes. It's just a matter of finding each of these.

Another way to find these is to ask the people who run each business if they have a homeschool group class. If they like the idea, they may ask you to spread the word and see if you can get enough interest to offer a class.

What is a Homeschool Convention?

How do I know all these things about homeschooling? Well, it's because I'm the smartest woman on the planet. Oh wait, no it isn't. The truth is, I've been to many years of homeschool conventions. Just like teachers in public schools have in-service days for professional development, homeschool parents do as well, it's called the homeschool convention.

Each summer there is a homeschool convention in every area of the country. At these events, they fill an entire auditorium with hundreds of homeschool curriculum vendors who can answer your questions, let you touch and flip through things and who will chat with your kids.

There are also famous keynote speakers like Ken Ham from The Creation Museum and Voddie Baucham. There are also smaller rooms with speakers on topics such as "how to homeschool your special needs child," "incorporating art into your homeschool," "the Montessori method," and "helping your right-brain learner understand math."

It's important to attend one of these as soon as possible. They will give you encouragement and insight as you gather with thousands of homeschool parents just like you.

You may think it's crazy to hear a homeschooling mom rave about a math curriculum, but once you've been to a homeschool convention and heard a speaker explain something that has confused you for years, you will rave too.

For the years that you can't make it to the convention, good homeschool magazine subscriptions like *The Old Schoolhouse* give a lot of great information.

Chapter 6

How Can I Make Sure my Homeschool is Successful?

We are not raising children, we are raising adults.

Think about the statement above. Your goal is not to raise large children who, at age 18, are trying to figure out how to be adults. Your goal is to slowly and steadily turn your infant into a prepared and successful adult. That is your goal. Never forget that.

Are You Saying You Run Your Home Like a Business?

Yes. Run your home like you're running a company. Make file folders for your bills, schoolwork you want to save, official documents, medical information and so forth.

Have a binder with tabs to keep any answer keys you pull out from the back of a workbook, printables you find online, a record of what each child has done that day and any lesson plans of what you hope to accomplish and when. A binder is also a great place to store any homeschool articles you like.

To keep daily records of what each child has done, you can purchase a beautiful planner or go to the dollar store and get a yearly planner. You can also search online for "free teacher planner." Write what each child does each day.

Here is an example of a family with kids aged 10, 5, and 3:

John- Science: p. 5-8
　　Math: lesson 8
　　Reading: "Charlotte's Web" chapter 2
　　Grammar: lesson 8
　　Spelling: list 1 review
　　History: chapter 2

Sally- Language: p.3
　　Math: p.3
　　Science: p.5-8

Ben- Dollar store workbook page
　　Build with blocks

"Help! I Just Pulled my Kids Out of School"

When you're homeschooling for the long term,
the thing about homeschooling is,
if you mess up one year,
you can fix it the next.

WHEN YOU'RE homeschooling for the short term, the pressure to keep up with the school system, no matter how flawed, will weigh heavily on you. It will affect how you choose curriculum and how hard you push your kids. This leads to a lot of excess stress. It does not lead to effective homeschooling.

I fluctuate one way or the other. One year I push hard for academic excellence, making formal education the top priority. At the end of that year, I realize that we've not done enough hands-on activities, field trips or group activities. So, the next year we do all the things we missed the previous year and I lighten up on the academics. At the end of that year, I realize we didn't go as in-depth into some subjects as I would have liked, so the next year we hit it hard and back and forth. The beauty of it is that I can course correct immediately. Did we join too many sports teams and are running around all over the place this year? Next year, we will commit to only one. Did we skip the Christmas or Valentine's Day party? We will make those events next year.

Balance comes when we put all the years together. It doesn't always happen in the moment. You're going to make mistakes. That's normal. But the mistakes you make will not be from lack of love for your children.

Don't neglect going to events, you need the community support even more than your kids do.

Remember: You're not trying to convince your children to love homeschooling. It will feel like it sometimes, but that's not your actual goal. You decided to homeschool because of the reasons you wrote down at the beginning of this book. Children make poor decisions regularly, like not bathing, wanting to eat candy for every meal or wanting to play in the street. The reasons you decided to homeschool have nothing to do with what your children want at that particular moment. If your son comes crying to you because he misses his friends and wants to go back to school, that is a hint that you need to find more social activities for him.

How Can I Know if I'm Doing it Right?

At first you won't know. You will just be getting used to everything and so will your kids. What you're looking for during the first six months is a change in attitude. Are your kids getting the routine down? Are they relaxing and feeling more comfortable in their own skin? Are they making friends? Are they learning to read for pleasure and getting to know the library?

Eventually you will be able to measure progress by seeing that in the beginning they struggled with 1+1 and now they are doing 12+12 easily.

Another way to check their progress is to order an at home test from Seton. Every few years I test my kids, just to see what the test says. Sometimes I learn a lot, sometimes it tells me what I already knew. To buy this test, go to SetonTesting.com and click on the "For Individuals" tab. Then go to "Standardized Tests" and "CAT Survey". Scroll down to test version and select "Survey" then choose your children's grade levels and order those. You don't need the test prep books or anything else. This is just for your own information. You can take the test once a year, once every few years, or at the beginning of the year and the end of the year to compare.

Over the past 17 years, I've watched hundreds of families pull their children out of school and begin homeschooling. When their child attends their first park day, they are often withdrawn and wearing clothing that was more of a protective shield in school. It's not unusual to see girls dressed in black or thick clothing on their first park day, but within a few months they are wearing pastel colors, laughing, and smiling. Seeing the tear-filled eyes of their parents as they watch their child turn back into themselves is awe inspiring.

You can also watch for new skills that your children develop. When they had limited time at home, did they learn how to cook? Now that they're home all day, you can make sure they learn how to make simple meals like quesadillas, spaghetti, scrambled eggs, macaroni and cheese, grilled cheese sandwiches, tacos, and baked potatoes. For a young child, reading a recipe could count as reading for the day. Following directions is an important skill to master and measuring ingredients is the practical application of the math skills they are learning.

What Can I do While Waiting for my Materials to Arrive?

Until your books arrive, you can go on field trips and there are excellent websites such as TeachersPayTeachers.com with thousands of printable activities to go with those field trips.

You can take a trip to the zoo and search online for "free zoo worksheet 6 grade" to print off something for each child to do following their zoo trip. The following day, you could head to the library and have each child get a book on the animal they liked the best. You could expand this into finding an Animal Planet program on this animal or an area of the world such as "animals of the tropics" or "nocturnal animals."

This would also be a great time to recreate some of your favorite memories from childhood, like making a diorama or creating a vinegar and baking soda volcano.

What is Deschooling?

If you think your children need to come down from the stress or trauma they encountered at school and "de-school" for the first 2-4 weeks, then your de-schooling routine might look like:

- Taking field trips
- Watching educational documentaries
- Assigning a research project

- Getting to know the library
- Visiting homeschool events, classes, and co-ops
- Reading The Tuttle Twins book series
- Watching the entire series of *Engineering an Empire, Liberty's Kids,* and *Drive Through History*

Vicki Says:

You may have heard the term *de-schooling* (this is not the same as *un-schooling*, which is a teaching approach—but some unschooling tips also work for de-schooling[8]). *De-schooling* refers to taking a period of time to allow your child to rediscover the wonder of learning. As explained in "Suddenly Homeschooling: The Basics,"[9]

"De-schooling is a fancy term for letting go of the old paradigm and realizing that homeschooling doesn't have to look like school at home. It may take a month or more to adjust to the idea of *facilitating your child's learning,* vs *schooling* him.

It's okay to let your kids de-school by simply reading, or learning about something they want to learn about, or taking some virtual field trips, or working on a hobby, or cooking with you, or doing a family project.

(Translation: Learning can still happen just in the context of being a family–so enjoy!)"

Remember that this is a transition for your child, too—not just academically, but socially and emotionally as well. His familiar routine—his security—has changed. Be patient with your child, and remember that this is new for him, too. He may not know how to handle the freedom; he may need you to guide him in what to do, and work gradually into more self-direction.

De-schooling is also an opportunity for you to rediscover the wonder of your family! When I consult with families, I try to help them get a sense of what their family vision is and what sorts of activities they enjoy, so we can endeavor to find a homeschool approach that's a good fit for who they are as a family. And when that happens, children are more likely to be willing participants in the learning process.

∽

Chapter 7

But Aren't Homeschooled Kids Uncool?

What About Socialization?

At first homeschool kids don't seem cool because they don't feel pressured to keep up with the latest trends or wear much makeup. Studies have shown that homeschoolers tend to have better interactions between age groups[16], so they are less likely to exclude new kids.

Newly homeschooled middle and high school kids are often stunted in interpersonal relationship building because of the public-school environment where walking up to a new person or group of kids doesn't go well at school.

For kids who have been homeschooled for several years, there is a stark difference. When new homeschoolers come to an event, I usually grab a child I know and ask them to introduce the new kid. They are happy to do it. I say,

"Janice, this is Erica. She's new to the group. Would you mind introducing her to the other girls?"

99% of the time this goes very well and the new child feels welcomed. The time or two when this hasn't happened it's usually because the new child will not interact with the other kids and alienates them. This can go away with time. They are just scared.

The homeschool environment is so different that generally by the next school year that new homeschooler is the one I ask to introduce another new person. It will feel like the first day at a new school or the first day at a new job. You'll hate it, but keep attending. Yes, the first couple of times you arrive at an event it's going to be uncomfortable for all of you.

You can help with this by going to the same events each week. If there is a weekly park date go to it rain or shine, whether you feel like it or not and even when your kids don't want to go. Your persistence will pay off. The first 5-6 times your children may not leave your side. They may refuse to talk with anyone, but at some point something unplanned will happen.

It could be that your pouty teen daughter drops her art supplies and another girl her age helps picks them up and says she liked to draw manga characters. Or your pre-teen son brings his skateboard and suddenly finds himself surrounded by eager little faces saying how cool his flips are. It only takes one good interaction for the feelings to change. Maybe the next week your son isn't fighting you as hard when you say it's time for park day. Maybe he even joins in when the other boys ask him to play football. It's a process, but if you persevere there can be a good outcome.

At the very least you can know that you've done all that you can to provide everything your children need educationally, spiritually, and socially.

And don't overlook church activities. If you aren't already going to churches, this is a great time to start. In fact, it's a great time to ask your fellow homeschoolers which church they go to. You may find that several go to the same church and it might be worth checking it out. There are often mid-week youth groups with great, safe, social activities where your children can form friendships.

I always planned to join Classical Conversations (CC) if we ever moved and had trouble finding a local homeschool group to join. I haven't encountered that problem, so we never joined, but CC has always looked like an attractive option.

If you struggle to find the interaction you are looking for, check out your local Classical Conversations. Even if it's not your preferred homeschool style, it could be a great place to form friendships for both you and your children.

If I Build it, Will They Come?

If you can't find the classes or activities you are looking for, set them up! There are several ideas below.

Playgroups
Co-ops
Classes

Field trips
Park days
Mom's night out
Holiday parties
Cooking classes
Animal care
Gardening
Farm skills
Zoo field trip
Museums
Fast food or bakery or candy making tours
Planetarium
College tours
Hiking
Pottery
Painting
Scavenger hunt
Fruit picking
Woodworking
Food pantry
Factory
Recycling center
Fire station
Google "homeschool field trip ideas"

Chapter 8

How do I Handle Hard Days?

It's okay to love what you're doing and still need a break.

You will hyperventilate at least twice a year and wonder if you're ruining your kids! You will question your ability to teach your children. You will wonder if they are getting all the social time and educational opportunities that they need. You will question your sanity. But you will have a moment the next week when you realize that this is working and that it's the right thing to do.

Children will rise to the level of your expectations. If they struggle with a subject, as homeschoolers, you can slow down to make sure they get it before moving on, just be sure you aren't setting the bar too low.

When my youngest struggled with math, I instituted a new prize system. Getting a 90% or higher on a math page would earn a visit to the prize box. To my surprise I found that the child who struggled in math could get an A when given a reason to focus. My child was more capable than I thought.

"Fool me once, shame on you. Fool me twice, shame on me."
-Italian Proverb

How to Have a Happy Homeschool

STEP #1- Stop trying to have a happy homeschool. That will put a lot of pressure on you. Homeschooling is like working out, cleaning your room, or eating your vegetables. It's not the fun part of life. You don't jump out of bed and think, "Yay, I can't wait to clean my room!" But you're much happier in a clean room. Homeschooling can be fun, but that's not the main goal. Your goal is to raise adults with the skills necessary to be successful in this world.

Step #2- Remember WHY you decided to homeschool. You didn't decide to homeschool because you couldn't imagine five minutes without your children. You did it because _____.

Step #3- If you can't find it, create it. I've seen a lot of parents complain when some activity doesn't exist. If you can't find a group class that your child wants, create it yourself. That's how the classes currently offered began.

Step #4- Realize what the homeschool community is and isn't. We are fellow travelers on the same journey you're

"Help! I Just Pulled my Kids Out of School"

on. Community is giving and taking in turns. Make sure you're giving as much as you are taking.

Step #5- Have some perspective. When I was a kid, I hated meatloaf. Yuck. I sat for a long time after dinner staring at cold meatloaf that I didn't want to eat. But now I sometimes crave meatloaf and have very warm, nostalgic feelings when I eat it. What my parents were doing was creating a foundation of good eating that would disappear in my early adult life but reappear as foundational when I had a family of my own.

You're doing the same.

You're creating an environment of learning, family and the things that are important to you (health, self-expression, individuality, self-sufficiency, independence, creativity.) While they may not jump out of bed excited to learn, you are giving them a foundation they will return to at some point.

Step #6- Stop comparing your worst day/week/year to someone's best moment. That happy homeschool family, with the matching hand-sewn outfits and their hand-ground wheat to make homemade bread, isn't perfect. They would probably tell you that if you asked. People post pictures and examples of their wins. They rarely post photos of the days when their kids are crying on the floor because they asked them to pick up a pencil.

This is a marathon. Some points are painful, but the results are worth it. Keep your eye on the prize!

Nina Elena

Vicki Says:

Fourteen-year-old Rachel—usually engaged in learning, an overachieving firstborn—stood at the top of the stairs and yelled at her mother, "I *hate* you! And I hate homeschooling! I hate being cooped up in this house all day with seven kids! When I'm eighteen, I'm out of here, and I'm never doing this to my kids, because you are ruining my life!"

Her mom was able to remove herself from the situation, to not take it personally, and (somehow!) calmly announced to the irate teen,

"I'm so sorry you are not happy right now, but it's not my job to make you happy. It's my job to do what God has called me to do with you. If Dad and I didn't believe one hundred percent that this was God wanted for you, we'd put you back in school in a heartbeat—because it would be so much easier!"

"But we're accountable to God for how we raise you. If you get married and have kids and choose not to homeschool, that's between you and your husband and God... but Dad and I will have to answer to God someday for how we raise you, and if we're making a mistake, we're

"Help! I Just Pulled my Kids Out of School"

making it as honestly as we know... so I love you, and we can talk a bit when you are calmer."

Her parents didn't waffle in their decision—because they knew their *why*. They knew that our *why* directs our *what* and our *how*. They intentionally made the hard call for long-term benefits, because that's what parents sometimes have to do.

Of course, they made a point of giving her as much ownership, as many choices, as they could and to let her pick materials, scheduling, and more. And when she was eighteen, she didn't leave. In fact, she stayed till she married at twenty. After sending her parents several thank-you notes. You can read the rest of her story in her guest post, "I Hated Homeschooling."[10] (*Spoiler: She now has five kids. Guess what she's done with them from birth? Yep, she homeschools! And she writes homeschool how-to articles and books and curriculum. And her husband works for a national homeschooling organization. God has such a sense of humor.*)

Sometimes being the parent isn't the battle on the stairs. Sometimes it's reminding the kids of the plan for the day. Or holding them accountable for their assignments or their commitment to a volunteer job or their household tasks.

It also helps to have a plan for the day or the week,[11] let them know what that plan is, and be clear about your standards. I'm not advocating dinging a bell to segue from one subject to the next, but kids generally find security in routine, in a plan or pattern or rhythm for the day, and in knowing the expectations. We can't exactly argue that they've missed the mark if we haven't provided a clear and reasonable target.

~

How do I Respond When Someone Objects to Homeschool?

First, remember what we talked about in chapter five. You don't have to explain your decision to anyone. However, it is nice to have something planned to respond to people who question you.

When someone asks why your kids aren't in school or asks if you homeschool, try to get a feel for their motivation. Are they putting their nose in your business or are they genuinely curious? My kids would tell anyone, anywhere, that they were homeschooled. I'm a more private person and if the person bagging my groceries asked if there is a school holiday, I would just smile politely and change the subject. My kids didn't do that. They'd answer loudly, "We're homeschooled!"

I'm glad they had confidence and didn't think it was anything to hide, but I really didn't want to have a homeschool conversation with everyone who asked. After my kids joyfully answered that they were homeschooled, the person would either let it go, because they were just making conversation, or they might ask a question. Many times, they would say that they wished they had homeschooled or that they knew someone who was homeschooled.

While these conversations can be burdensome, I'm sure it's the friends and family who question your decision who are the hardest to answer.

If you hear comments such as:

"Oh, I could never homeschool."

"How do you handle having your kids home *all day*?"

"Aren't you worried about socialization?"

Grab a 3x5 card and write a version of this to keep in your purse:

> You're right, it's a sacrifice, but one our family is willing to make. We don't want our children to grow up thinking pedophilia is okay or that it's normal to have mass shooter drills or have their health and mental well-being determined by whatever the Governor decides is "the science" that week. Their minds and health are too important. Did you know that a huge percentage of public-school teachers send their kids to private school? Even they don't want their kids subjected to government school. On average, homeschoolers test one to two grades above their public-school peers. We are making the sacrifice now to help our kids have the best possible future.

There has been a meme going around the homeschool community, it takes the things people say to homeschool families and turns it around.

"Oh, I could never public school."

"How do you handle having your kids gone *all day*?"

"Aren't you worried about socialization?"

"I hope you know what you're doing."

"Are you qualified to choose a public school?"

"I met a public-school kid once, and they were weird. Is your child going to be weird?"

How do I Homeschool Multiple Kids at the Same Time?

Most homeschooling families have multiple children, so they will be your greatest resource. Posting a question on your local homeschool Facebook group or asking moms at homeschool events for advice will give you insight into how each family accomplishes this.

I can remember homeschooling in the hallway when our youngest was a toddler. Many families do this. They put the youngest child or two in their own room and put a baby gate across the door. Then the mom sits at the baby gate and teaches the other children who are laying or sitting in the hallway. This way, the toddler is contained, and the siblings can concentrate without a little sibling grabbing their paper or pencil.

You will also make use of your highchair and playpen during this age. Putting your toddler in their highchair and giving them toys or activities to play with while you work with your older children works well. Clipping toys to the tray so they can't be thrown off is also helpful.

Take advantage of nap time. When they wake up put

on an educational program while they are in the playpen if you need more time to work with your older kids.

It's also a great idea to put away some toys your toddlers and preschoolers like to play with so that you are bringing out different toys each week. This will help them be excited to play with them. Learning toys like Lincoln Logs, Legos, wooden blocks and wood puzzles are great items for them to use while you are teaching. If you pull out the Legos one week and then put those away and pull out the wooden blocks the next week, you'll have better luck keeping them occupied.

When you're teaching multiple school-aged children, it's helpful to use curriculum that is designed for multiple ages. Sonlight does a particularly good job at creating a curriculum that can teach multiple ages at once. "Teaching multiple students is easy with Sonlight curriculum packages. Combine students within a 3-year age range into one History / Bible / Literature level and one Science program. Then, simply add on skill-specific subjects for each child, according to ability..."[17]

Can I Homeschool my Child with Special Needs?

Absolutely, in fact you can keep your IEP and still get services while you homeschool. How you do this and what services you can get are beyond the scope of this book. I can direct you to your statewide homeschool support organization and HSLDA for assistance. To find your state homeschool organization, search online with the name of your state and the words "homeschool support," "network" or "organization", like this, "Arizona homeschool network".

If you have a child who is struggling or has special needs, Dianne Craft is the specialist to check out. Her resources are recommended by almost every homeschool convention. I've included a link to her website at NinaHelpsYouHomeschool.com.

Her website has a free one-hour video where she covers Tourette's, dyslexia, dysgraphia, ADHD, behavioral issues, learning issues, trouble sitting still, language issues, balance issues, trouble with learning sight-words and raising gifted children.

Her video is a must-watch for every homeschooling parent.

There is also a company called Thinking Tree Books that makes the Fun-Schooling curriculum. These workbooks are great for moms with chronic illness, children with dyslexia or dysgraphia and things for kids to do when you're sick.

The font in the books is made especially for kids with dyslexia and inside the books are things for the kids to do by themselves. You should look through these books to understand just how they work.

Let me remind you that the workbooks at the store labeled "comprehensive curriculum" are *not* homeschool curriculum. These are review or busywork. They don't actually teach the concepts.

Will I Ever Have "Me Time" Again?

If you get stuck and think you need to put your children back in school, reach out to your local homeschool group. There is usually someone who is available to talk you off the edge. It's tough work. I can't tell you how many times I've grabbed the phone and when my friend Sue answered the phone, instead of hearing "hello" all she heard was, "Talk me down!" We would each vent about our homeschool day and end up laughing and refreshed and go back to teaching with a smile on our faces. You need a friend like Sue.

It's not always easy, but it's always worth it. With this community around you, you're never alone, even when it feels like it.

I need "me time" that's why I get up at 5am every weekday. That gives me two hours in the morning to myself. I also want "me time" in the evening. The way I explain it to my family is, "After 14 hours together, I need some alone time. After 8pm I'm tired and grumpy." You can also use the words, "After ___pm I can't be a good mom." This helps your kids to understand that they need to let you have your own time to decompress after being patient all day.

You can make that time whatever works for you. Some days it may be the moment your husband walks in the door, other days it could be after 7pm.

What you're saying is that if the kids don't stay in bed at night or if they keep coming in to interrupt your time of peace and quiet, you won't be able to respond with love and care.

It's a nice way to express that mommy needs to replenish her cup of patience and kindness.

This doesn't mean that you don't love your family or that homeschooling is too much for you to handle. It just means that after a long day of being patient and kind, your cup is empty.

Once your family gets used to it, it will be easy to set this time aside. You can experiment and find out what this replenishing time looks like for you. It could be a bath, a book, an uninterrupted phone call with a friend, a walk, a movie with your husband, or sitting outside.

It's normal to feel overwhelmed sometimes.

It's normal to feel smothered sometimes.

It's normal to feel like you're failing sometimes.

It's okay to take some time to refill your cup.

If you need a break during the week and can't afford or find a class or group, find another homeschool mom and make a plan to swap kids for two hours a week. If there is something you love to do like teach art, make crafts, teach music or science, offer to do that once a week with her kids and then have her do what she loves once a week with yours. You will each get a break.

Vicki Says:

I'll be honest. There are days I just don't feel like doing the dishes. I may balk at getting started. I may dread taking the time. But eventually common sense (or the idea of having to do two days' worth tomorrow!) wins, and I talk myself into doing the responsible thing and getting them done.

Some days, our kids are like that. It's just been a long day, or they are interested in something else right now, or they dread getting started. (This is a normal scenario on occasion in many homeschool settings. It really isn't just your kiddo!) But our hope is that eventually they will realize that putting it off now just makes it tougher later, so they buckle down and cooperate.

∼

What if my Child Can't Focus?

To have the best school day possible, make sure breakfast is high in protein and has no sugar or gluten. Sugar and gluten cause brain fog and sugar crashes. This is easy to do by making eggs with bacon.

Keep a glass of water available all day to break a bad mood or help with concentration.

An example of this is when Billy breaks down over his fifth math problem and you repeat the problem to him through clenched teeth. You can quickly change the mood by changing your tone and saying, "Oh, wait, you haven't had a drink of water yet. Go grab some."

Sometimes this simple trick of diverting attention away from the problem by getting Billy to move out of his seat will work. Having a cool drink of refreshing water to replenish his dehydrated brain and body will also help.

On hard days, imagine you're Batman and pretend you have a "focusing tool belt." Use the same tactic as with the water, but this time have him get a piece of sugarless gum or trail mix, celery and peanut butter, carrots and dressing, string cheese or nuts. The final tool in your focusing tool belt is an essential oil roller, like doTERRA's "Motivation" blend. Again, you'll distract him with, "Oh, I know what we need, we forgot to use our motivation roller!"

Having these tools to pull out when things are tough is empowering for you and your child. He probably doesn't even know why he's in such a grumpy mood. You're helping him see that there are things he can do to snap himself out of a bad mood.

You can also set a goal like, "two more problems and then we're going outside!" Or, "As soon as we finish math, we can head to the park."

One thing I would caution you about is quitting school for the day when your child is having a bad day. The reason that you don't want to do this very often is because you are giving them a reason to have a bad day. We want to reward the behaviors we want to see repeated, not unacceptable behaviors. If every time our children have a bad day we put away the school work and do what they want to do, then we're teaching them to have bad days to get free time. That doesn't mean that you can't ever close the books on a bad day. We just need to be careful about the lessons we teach our children. They watch everything we do. If they see dad working hard to support his family, they will be like that when they grow up. If they see that it's fine to quit when things get hard, they will learn that too.

What if I Only Have One Child?

When you have one child at home, getting them out of the house to be with other kids is more important. You'll have to prioritize this in ways that families with six kids don't need to. Their kids always have a playmate in the house, yours doesn't.

While socialization isn't the primary concern of your homeschool, it is a valid concern when you have an only child. If there are plenty of kids in the neighborhood that your child is already friends with, then you may not need to make the extra effort. If this is not the case, then you'll need to sign up for more field trips, more park days, and more activities so your child will have plenty of friends in the homeschool group. Even with after-school friends, your child would benefit from having friends who are available during the day for last-minute activities.

Parents of only children must work harder at creating social time for their kids. That's the only real difference between homeschooling multiple children and homeschooling an only child.

What do I Teach at Each Stage?

Lost Tools of Learning Chart

Grades K-2	Grades 3-7
Pre-Polly	**Poll-Parrot**
• Excited about learning • Enjoys playing games, hearing stories, songs and projects • Has a short attention span • Likes to copy & imitate • Needs to touch, smell, taste, feel, see • Is imaginative & creative	• Likes to explain and figure things out • Excited about new and interesting facts • Relates his own exeriences to the subject • Likes to collect and organize things • Likes to repeat rhymes & chants • A great time to learn a new language
How to Teach	**How to Teach**
• Explore & find things • Hands-on learning • Build, color, draw, sing, play games • Short, creative projects • Repeat stories back to you • Field trips • Give copying and imitating opportunities	• Make collections, displays & models • Lessons should weave through subjects & senses • Teach and assign simple projects • Drama, memorization, repeating, chants, songs • Drills & games • Oral presentations • Field trips

@2023 Nina Elena, adapted from Tom Garfield

Grades 7-9	Grades 10-12
Pert	**Poetic**
<ul><li>Likes to debate, judge, critique and is critical of things</li><li>Likes to show off his knowledge</li><li>Likes to organize things and people</li><li>Wants to know "why"</li><li>Thinks is smarter than adults</li><li>Excited but wants to be challenged</li><li>Likes "insider" knowledge</li></ul>	<ul><li>Idealistic</li><li>Interested in current events and his own life</li><li>Concerned with justice and fairness</li><li>Developing special interests/hobbies</li><li>Can work independently and take on responsibility</li><li>Expresses his own feelings & ideas</li></ul>
How to Teach	**What to Teach**
<ul><li>Debates & persuasive reports</li><li>Guest speakers & trips</li><li>Collaborative work in groups</li><li>Time lines, maps, charts & other visual material</li><li>Drama, role-play and reenactments of events</li><li>Evaluate & critique</li><li>Learn rules of logic</li><li>Research projects & presentations</li></ul>	<ul><li>Classic literature, history, speeches & debate</li><li>Write papers & discuss his worldview</li><li>Construct a public defense of a thesis</li><li>Expore drama & poetry & giving oral presentations</li><li>Learn how to research and present cohesive ideas</li><li>Added responsibilities</li><li>Field trips</li></ul>

Chapter 9

Is it Possible to Homeschool my High Schooler?

Kids don't understand why it's happening, but they sense themselves being put to death in school. That's why they hate it so much. -John Taylor Gatto

What Challenges Does High School Present?

High school can be one of the most rewarding times to homeschool. Your teens are beginning to venture into the world and are becoming adults. They have thoughts and opinions to share and will often amaze you with their insights.

This is also a time when peer pressure in public and private schools is the most dangerous. It's not always pressure to do a particular thing, but pressure to disappear into the background. High schoolers feel like they have a giant target on their backs and one wrong move will bring unwanted attention from the crowd.

While hormones can make some high schoolers emotional, being there for their emotional and educational needs is important. They need a stable adult to discuss their plans with, a shoulder to cry on and help them navigate working outside the home.

One way to engage your high school children and get their buy-in is to get them involved in the process. You can do this by getting the Christian Book Distributor's homeschool catalog and handing it to them. Tell them you've already picked out their math and language programs but that you'd like them to help choose the science program that looks good to them. The CBD catalog has a collection of different homeschool curriculum so your kids can see a variety and a brief description of each.

Alternately, you can narrow it down to two science programs that you like and say, "I've found these two science programs. I'd like you to have more control over your education. Which one do you like best?"

You can also get creative. One year, I gave my oldest a copy of the table of contents from a biology textbook and said to use her artistic skills to make her own textbook that covered these topics. Using a composition notebook, she created her own version of a textbook with research done at the library and her own drawings. This was perfect for her learning style.

A lot of times I talk to parents about teaching high school

and they say, "Well, I know my child isn't going to college." While you may know this about your child, if possible, set them up for success at college anyway. You can do this by looking at the graduation requirements for your state. If your state only requires 3 years of math to graduate, but your local college requires 4 years of math, it's better to do the 4 years. This way they can enter college with no problems. Without this, they may have to take remedial classes or have trouble being admitted into certain universities.

Children will rise to the level of your expectations.

Not every child can handle the course load of a typical high school student.

Each child has a specific set of needs and if one of your children has a learning disability, then simply graduating with the skills he needs will be a success. However, make sure that you're not shortchanging your children just because it's easier than fighting them to get an excellent education. If you know why a good education is necessary, then putting in the extra effort will be easier.

You can also involve your high school or junior high children by sitting down with them and asking some questions.

- What things do you want to do this year? (Get a job? Learn to drive? Go to camp? Learn to code?)

- What do you want to do when you graduate? (Go to college? Go to work? Graduate early?)
- What are you interested in? (Video games? Photography? Fashion? News reporting?)
- How can we help you make those things happen? (Go get your permit from the DMV? Get a part-time job to earn money for camp? Find a good English program so you can become a reporter?)

After several months of high school, visit your local community college's website to find out about entry requirements and dual enrollment options.

How do I Create a High School Plan?

The biggest difference between homeschooling in elementary school and homeschooling in high school is that there may be requirements to graduate. You can find these by searching for the name of your state and "department of education graduation requirements."

You may not need to follow these requirements exactly so you should visit HSLDA and your statewide homeschool support group for correct information. Do not directly contact your local school, the state, or a college for information.

Non-homeschool organizations often give out wrong information. In fact I can almost guaranteed you'll get bad information if you ask any of them. Hundreds of homeschooling families have been told that their child can't enroll in a college class or their diploma doesn't count or other wrong information simply because the person they spoke to didn't have accurate information. If you are a member of HSLDA and this happens to you, then you can contact HSLDA and they will help resolve the issue.

HIGH SCHOOL USUALLY REQUIRES:

- Language arts (4 years) American literature/composition, British literature/composition, world literature/composition, speech/communication
- Math (3–4 years) algebra 1 & 2, geometry, pre-calculus/trigonometry
- Social studies (3–4 years) world history, American history, United States government
- Science (3–4 years) physical science, earth science, biology, chemistry
- Foreign language (2–4 years)
- Physical education (1–2 years)
- Fine arts (1–2 years) art, music, drama, dance
- Electives (6 classes) Bible, coding, woodworking, auto mechanics

Can my Kids Officially Graduate and go to College?

Absolutely. The diploma you give your child and the transcripts you make for them are valid to present to colleges for admission. If you would like to have official-looking graduation materials, HSLDA has beautiful diplomas, caps, gowns, national honor society stoles and more.

HomeLife Academy (Homelifeacademy.com) is another terrific resource for homeschool families. HomeLife essentially acts as the buffer between you and anyone who thinks that homeschool isn't "real school." You input the classes you are teaching each year and the materials you are using, along with the grades your child earns. They create an official transcript each year and when graduation comes, they make a diploma for you.

We have used both HSLDA and HomeLife Academy at various times in our homeschool journey. One perk of using an "umbrella school" such as HomeLife is that if anyone intrusive asks where your child goes to school, you can answer, "Oh, HomeLife Academy."

Vicki Bentley has written extensively about high school planning and creating high school transcripts for your children. I own some of the resources she has available at EverydayHomemaking.com.

"Help! I Just Pulled my Kids Out of School"

Vicki Says:

Once your kids are middle school-ish or above, their *I don't want to* can be not only *I can't,* but also *I'm bored* or *I'm miserable* or *I'm never going to use this, so why bother?*

Let's be honest. Do you really want to do something for hours a day, every day, just because someone else tells you what to do, how to do it, and when to do it? You probably want to have some choice in what and when and how. And you want it to be relevant to your life, one way or another. If not, it's simply busywork.

Maybe your teen doesn't want to learn math, but he *does* want to start a lawn care business or paint his room or design a video game or be able to figure out if his future paycheck is correct or his investments are wise. If he can see that he will need those math skills—even if he isn't thrilled about learning them—you have salted his proverbial "oats" and now he's thirsty! Learning is now relevant.

For our teens, motivation, perseverance, and diligence are often linked to relevance and choices.[12] If removing that math course from the equation doesn't add up for your student's plan right now (see what I did there?), can you give him a choice in which course he takes? Can you let him choose between online or text or in-person class? Can he decide whether he does it first thing in the morning or late at night? Choices empower our students to take ownership of their learning. You can minimize the power struggle by giving your student as much autonomy as he shows he can handle.

Chapter 10

What Else do I Need to Know?

John Taylor Gatto made a list of things he felt education should produce. While his list is meant to be read to a senate committee, this shortened version will give you an idea of what he thought education should look like.

I'll paraphrase:

- Educated people don't have trouble finding something to do and don't mind being alone.
- Educated people understand people so they have good relationships and interactions.
- Educated people understand their life is temporary and try to learn from those around them.
- Educated people are aware of the values and

cultures of the world and have formed their own set of values to live by.
- Educated people love to create new things and discover truth through exploration and evidence.
- Educated people notice other people's needs and find a way to meet those needs in a way that produces well-paid work and employment. They also realize that love, curiosity, honor and empathy don't cost money and produce happiness.
- Educated people seek variety. They find pleasure and knowledge in different things, but understand that without a home and responsibilities, variety is empty.
- Educated people ask themselves the deep questions like; Who am I? Where are my limits? What am I capable of? Which version of myself do I show in each situation?
- Educated people examine the physical world, study, investigate, and test it.
- Educated people wrestle with family relationships, friendships, companionships, comradeship, love, hate, community, and networking.
- Educated people contemplate the best way to contribute to the common good while simultaneously earning a living doing so.
- Educated people study death, the final act of

life, realizing they are mortal and that leaving a legacy to the next generation is powerful.

Think back to your high school or jr. high years. Do you start to smile? Are there some great friends and memories you have from that time?

Now, take a minute and think back, were you ever pressured to do something you didn't want to do? Did you ever feel scared or intimidated? Did you ever have anyone bring a handgun or drugs to school? Did you ever have to look over your shoulder to make sure no one came up behind you? Did anyone ever bully you? How was the locker room? Were there any weird teachers? When did you feel unsafe? How did you feel at the sporting events you attended? Who was your enemy? Why did he or she hate you?

The reason I ask you these questions is to help you remember the truth about school. We often have a rosy picture of our past, remembering only the best parts, then we expose our children to the *real* situation.

Your child may do the same. She may forget the boy who tripped her and pulled her hair, but she remembers the one time her friend shared her birthday cookie with her. She misses this. What she doesn't realize yet is that there are a dozen girls her age who are homeschooled and who would love to be her friend. These new friends will invite her to their birthday parties, include her, make her feel special and will be a safe space for her and for you. There is something better out there. And they won't judge her based on what she's wearing or if she's cool enough.

You'll have to push through the hard parts of that first year. Don't worry too much about how your children feel in the moment, knowing that your decision will have a positive outcome in the long run.

Remember why you decided to homeschool.

- What were your concerns?

- What did you see your children encounter?

- What incident happened?

- What bad things happened to other kids and families at the school?

How Can I Learn from Your Mistakes?

I mentioned earlier that I didn't buy the first-grade teacher's guide. I passed first grade, so how hard could it be to teach it? Wrong. I was scrambling to explain things like why a vowel was silent. This made our school day disjointed when I had to stop and find items to explain each concept. The teacher's guide would have told me exactly how to explain the concepts, instead of having to do it on my own. I kicked myself for doing that, especially when I saw how great the teacher's guides were.

Another mistake I made was that I made a school room.

Yes, I thought it was going to be so much fun to have a room dedicated to school. Yes, I was stuck in one room when I could have been getting things done around the house while waiting for my kids to do their schoolwork.

Kids do what you inspect, not what you expect.

I also didn't know that my children would go through phases and one of those phases was being untrustworthy. You may need to lock up your answer keys. There are plastic boxes at Walmart or office supply stores and you can get a lock there as well.

One thing I learned was that our children weren't vending machines. Just because I put in three quarters, didn't mean that was going to get a drink. No matter how much you invest in your children, they are still individuals. They are responsible for their own choices, just like you and I. Our job is to present them with opportunities, but it is up to them to take advantage of them. They will make poor choices. We all do. They can bounce back, but their resiliency largely depends on what we've poured into them when they were young.

My children, Vicki's children, and the children you read about in chapter one are just a few examples of the results of homeschooling. It's a beautiful way to raise the next generation and gives me hope for the future. I hope your homeschool journey is everything you dream it can be.

Nina Elena

Vicki Says:

On the challenging days, remember Paul's words:

"Therefore, my beloved brethren, be steadfast, immovable, always abounding in the work of the Lord, knowing that your labor is not in vain in the Lord." 1 Corinthians 15:58 NKJV

And it doesn't hurt to print this one out—nice and big—for the refrigerator door, where the kids can see it.

"Obey your leaders and submit to them, for they are keeping watch over your souls, as those who will have to give an account. Let them do this with joy and not with groaning, for that would be of no advantage to you." Hebrews 13:17 ESV

As I type, I'm praying for you who are now reading this. May you find strength, patience, provision, wisdom, direction, and joy in the Lord who has called you to home discipleship of your precious children.

Chapter 11

Preview of The Next Book, "Help! I Need Some Homeschool Tips"

Some weeks I meal plan, making sure everyone gets three solid meals per day, other weeks I instill and nurture survival skills. Follow me for more homeschool hacks.
-Facebook Meme

If you're having a hard time getting through all the subjects you had hoped to cover this year, have no fear! There's a simple trick to getting through more subjects in less time. I call it bathroom learning.

Yes, our children learn in the bathroom.

The trick to bathroom learning is not to say anything about it. To begin, put a magazine holder by the toilet. One year, I wanted to cover marine biology, but we had too much going on to fit that in. Bathroom learning came to the rescue! I put Usborne books on marine mammals in the magazine holder along with brochures from the aquarium and pamphlets from our trip to Oahu. Voila!

One more place to fill our children's minds with knowledge.

Another way to utilize the bathroom is to put classroom posters across from the toilet. Stapling a poster of the ladybug life cycle or the sign language alphabet to the wall is a great way to help your children learn that information. You can also write Bible verses and inspirational sayings on the bathroom mirror.

I learned the bathroom trick from the book *Cheaper by the Dozen* by Frank B. Gilbreth. In the book they painted the Morse Code in their beach house bathroom and by the end of the summer every member of the family had it memorized.

The bathroom is a great place for educational items you find at the dollar store or at garage sales. Don't put expensive books in the bathroom because the humidity and accidental spills may ruin them.

This same tactic works with placemats at the table. You can get educational placemats that cover everything: presidents of the United States, telling time, the Constitution, math facts, the periodic table, or the sign language alphabet.

You can also make a to-go bag with educational toys, books and Mad Libs to take with you to doctor appointments. Usually these are things that my kids wouldn't pick up if there was any other entertainment available.

Mad Libs are great books to put in the car. It doesn't matter if the drive is long or short, there's always time for Mad Libs. Again, the beauty of this is that while your kids think they are making a funny story, they are actually learning the parts of speech. Mad Libs will teach them adverbs, nouns, verbs, and adjectives.

It's amazing to see the information they absorb from these little tricks. Your children will sound intelligent and none of these things add more work to your school day.

IF YOU'VE ENJOYED *HELP! I Just Pulled my Kids Out of School*, please tell people about it on social media. I also invite you to leave a review at Amazon, Barnes & Noble, or Goodreads. Reviews help others know that a book is worth reading. Share a tip you learned in your review.

To find the resources mentioned and get notified about the next book, visit NinaHelpsYouHomeschool.com.

Afterword: Can You Just Tell me What to do?

If you'd like personalized help designing your homeschool plan or if you've been homeschooling for a while and would like some additional guidance, you can use the form at NinaHelpsYouHomeschool.com to book a consultation.

Sample Consult with the Author

This is a consultation I did for a family who pulled their children out of public school several months prior to our talk. This family's situation was quite complex. Beatrice (7th grade) had severe medical issues that took her out of school for months every year. This meant that she had missed so many basic concepts in her education that there was no way to keep up. She also loved art and struggled with dyslexia. Jeanie (1st grade) was a bright and engaged child, but her education had not kept up with how smart she was. Shawn

(8th grade) was a fair student but hated reading and language arts. Christopher (10th grade) just wanted to be done with school and go to work, but his math ability was behind.

What you can expect from a child who has been homeschooled from early elementary through junior high and what you can expect from a child who has just been taken out of public school is very different. Parents are learning how to assign schoolwork as well, so my recommendations are based on the habits of the entire family.

I am also looking for important gaps in each child's education. If they don't know how to sound out words, then we need to go back to that point and give that child the foundation he or she needs. It doesn't matter if they are in high school. It's the same with every subject.

Jeanie age 6 (public school 1st grade):

Abeka full grade K5 unaccredited video curriculum with books. This will set her up for being a strong reader, an excellent student, and she will know every subject very well. You'll enjoy seeing how it's done and after using it for a year you can decide if next year you want to do the video instruction with the books or just the books. Abeka is advanced, so getting K5 should be perfect for her even though she's in 1st grade. It will give her all the basics and will also give her big sister a better foundation as she overhears the lessons. It is more expensive than simply buying textbooks, but they usually offer a discount for new families. Ask Abeka if there is a new student discount when you order.

Beatrice (age 12, public school 7th grade):

History, *Fashion Dreams 1800-2030 Time Travel History* (This is the Fun Schooling brand drawing workbook, with special dyslexia typeface.)

Geography, *Travel Dreams Geography Seven Amazing Continents*

Science—do this with Shawn using his science book (you or Shawn can read the science book to Beatrice) and then she and Shawn can do the experiments together.

Math—Abeka *Arithmetic* 3 student workbook and teacher key (for you)

Language—Spectrum Language Arts Grade 3 student workbook (buy 2 one for Beatrice and one for Shawn, the answer key is in the back of the book, just tear it out when it arrives)

Shawn (age 14, public school 8th grade):

Science, Introductory Dissection Kit—(buy two kits, one for Shawn, one for Beatrice) and one textbook of Abeka *Investigating God's World* for Shawn to read to himself (then have him tell you about what he read each day after he's done reading several pages)

History—Abeka *History of the US* (have both boys share the textbook this year)

Abeka *History of the US* workbook (buy two, one for Shawn and one for Christopher)

(There is a teacher key for the Abeka *History of the US* book and also for the workbook. You can buy these if you want the answer keys.)

Math—Teaching Textbooks (available as a computer program online, should have an assessment on the website to see which grade to get)

Language Arts—Spectrum Language Arts Grade 3

Christopher (age 16, public school 10th grade):

To graduate he needs- 2 years of physical education (PE) 180 hours each year, Biology 101, Physics 101, 1 year of US History with Geography, 1 year of World History with Geography, ½ a year of American Government and ½ a year of Civics. He needs 2 years of math. This can be consumer math one year, but he must pass Algebra 1 to graduate. He must take 3 years of English and one year of a career tech or performing arts class to graduate.

I suggest this year he takes:

PE (get as many hours in as you can and keep track of them)

Abeka American History and Geography (use the same book as Shawn and buy each boy a maps workbook)

Math, Teaching Textbooks (take the online assessment to see where he fits and buy that course)

English, Learning Language Arts Through Literature (LLATL) Gold Book (The answer key is in the back of the book. Just remove it when it arrives)

Next year, 11th grade:

Biology 101: Biology According to the Days of Creation

PE (180 hours)

Abeka World History and Geography (and workbook)

Math (either Consumer Math, Algebra 1, or whatever he needs to get Algebra 1 completed before graduation)

English, Learning Language Arts Through Literature (LLATL) World Literature

12th grade:

Physics 101: The Mechanics of God's Physical World

½ a year of American Government

½ a year of Civics

Algebra 1

PE (finish however many hours are needed to finish 10th grade's 180 hours)

English, Learning Language Arts Through Literature (LLATL) British Literature

He will still need one year of a foreign language, performing arts or career technical education. (You can figure this out when you get to his senior year.)

Sample Consult With a Single Mom

Another consultation was for a single, working mom who pulled her child out of public school in the 9th grade. This family's situation was also different because the mom was working all day and had dyslexia. This meant she wouldn't have the time to teach her child, and grading was going to be difficult for her.

For this situation, I recommended she use Accelerated Christian Education (ACE) that first year for every subject except math.

ACE isn't a curriculum I recommend often. It worked well for this mom because she needed something in print, so her child was not on the computer, while he was with her all day at the office. She also needed something that taught itself. The ACE curriculum accomplished both goals.

Math could be done on the computer at home each evening.

I hope you've enjoyed this book and feel empowered to take your child's education into your own hands. With love and a willingness to learn, you are fully capable of helping them excel.

About the Author

After 17 years of homeschooling their children, Nina and her husband have two happy adult kids and one not yet graduated. All three children have different personalities and strengths.

Nina has also homeschooled special needs foster children, created homeschool support groups, been a homeschool speaker, mentored new homeschool moms, owned a home business and is a bestselling author under another name.

Acknowledgments

Thank you Vicki, Rebecca, Jessica and Laura for contributing your voices to *Help!* I'm grateful to the entire team at Zamiz Press for making this book a success.

Recommended Reading

Recommended Reading for Homeschool Parents

- *Weapons of Mass Instruction* by John Taylor Gatto
- *The Vanishing American Adult* by Ben Sasse
- *The Read-Aloud Handbook* by Jim Trelease
- *The Power of Habit* by Charles Duhigg
- *Atomic Habits* by James Clear
- *Outliers* by Malcolm Gladwell
- *The Underground History of American Education: Volume One* by John Taylor Gatto
- *Blackout* by Candace Owens
- *The Lost Tools of Learning* by Dorothy Sayers

Additional Reading

- *Battle for the American Mind* by Pete Hegseth
- *Atlas Shrugged* by Ayn Rand
- *Over the Top* by Zig Ziglar
- *Failing Forward* by John Maxwell
- *The Tipping Point* by Malcolm Gladwell

Endnotes

Endnotes

1. Baltimore: https://www.theblaze.com/news/zero-students-proficient-in-math-in-23-baltimore-schools-test-results-reveal?fbclid=IwAR2_uUlpc3ByTBKO7TePqC58n-VFCvLMjMSJt-aKYSxIKjJp2dAQPvuiaWk#toggle-gdpr
2. Ukraine: https://republicanwatch.com/ukrainian-refugee-wants-to-leave-after-two-months-in-san-francisco/?fbclid=IwAR3XPkmgFmO6IZahQnWOzk6d1Bz86XcTJenGiGcporbu2Cshn9J_QoyVizQ
3. San Francisco: https://www.sfexaminer.com/news/education/another-sf-middle-school-falls-

into-disciplinary-chaos/article_468ccbce-9095-11ed-a69c-1b42852679ae.html
4. Dr. Susan Berry: https://www.aop.com/blog/why-colleges-are-recruiting-homeschoolers
5. Peterson, Jordan. *12 Rules for Life*. Random House Canada, 2018.
6. Ziglar, Zig. *Over the Top*. 2nd ed., Thomas Nelson, 1997.
7. Fast growing: https://projects.propublica.org/graphics/homeschool
8. Legality: https://hslda.org/post/answers-to-your-most-pressing-homeschooling-questions
9. Gatto, John Taylor. *Weapons of Mass Instruction*. New Society Publishers, 2009.
10. Department of Education: https://nces.ed.gov/pubs2017/2017102.pdf
11. *Battle for the American Mind,* Pete Hegseth, Harper Collins 2022 [Quote emphasis mine]
12. "Character." Merriam-Webster.com Dictionary, Merriam-Webster, https://www.merriam-webster.com/dictionary/character. Accessed 20 Apr. 2023.
13. Charlotte Mason: https://simplycharlottemason.com
14. Susan Wise Bauer: https://welltrainedmind.com/a/classical-education/
15. Classical education: https://classicalacademicpress.com/pages/what-is-classical-education

Endnotes

16. Social interaction: https://www.nheri.org/a-systematic-review-of-the-empirical-research-on-selected-aspects-of-homeschooling-as-a-school-choice/
17. Sonlight: https://www.sonlight.com/homeschool/curriculum

Elliot Tanner: https://www.theepochtimes.com/after-2-years-homeschooling-using-high-school-curriculum-boy-13-graduates-college-with-3-78-gpa_4468991.html?ea_src=open&ea_med=search

Kip & Mona Lisa Harding: https://www.theepochtimes.com/brainy-bunch-parents-homeschool-their-10-kids-with-all-of-them-graduating-high-school-at-12_4210059.html?ea_src=ai&ea_med=search

Lost Tools of Learning: https://logosschool.com/wp-content/uploads/2011/09/LOST-TOOLS-CHART.pdf

Cover quotes are taken from: https://omny.fm/shows/the-charlie-kirk-show/when-we-removed-god-from-school-with-pete-hegseth

Share your favorite resources with the author.

Endnotes

"Vicki Says" Endnotes

1. Robin Sampson, *The Heart of Wisdom Teaching Approach*, Heart of Wisdom Publishing, 2005
2. Bentley, "Life is Messy," https://everydayhomemaking.com/life-is-still-messy/
3. Bentley, "Jump-start to Joyful Motherhood," Alliance Recordings, https://www.alliancerecordings.com/detail.cfm?context=Recordings&SpeakerID=27&RID=2174
4. Bentley, "Is My Child Ready to Read?" https://everydayhomemaking.com/is-my-child-ready-to-read
5. Ginny Yurich, "Play is the Main Occupation of Children," 1000 Hours Outside, https://www.1000hoursoutside.com/blog/play-is-the-main-occupation-of-children-interview-with-angela-hanscom
6. Bentley, "What to Do with Your Young Learner," https://everydayhomemaking.com/what-to-do-with-your-young-learner/

Endnotes

7. Rebekah McBride, Strewing article https://nodeskrequired.com/what-is-strewing
8. Rachel Ramey, "Unschooling—What Inspires Learning?" Titus 2 Homemaker, https://titus2homemaker.com/unschooling-what-inspires-learning/
9. Vicki Bentley, "Suddenly Homeschooling: The Basics," Everyday Homemaking, https://everydayhomemaking.com/SuddenlyHomeschooling-TheBasics
10. Rachel Ramey, "I Hated Homeschooling," Everyday Homemaking, https://everydayhomemaking.com/i-hated-homeschooling/
11. Bentley, "Suddenly Homeschooling: The Basics" https://everydayhomemaking.com/SuddenlyHomeschooling-TheBasics
12. Bentley, "Making the Most of the Middle School Years," https://everydayhomemaking.com/making-the-most-of-the-middle-school-years/

Editor's Note

As I edited this book, I thought about how much I relished the time with my now adult children. We went everywhere together. That was the gift—the gift of time with my favorite people. I had a front-row seat when they struggled and when they had their light bulb moments.

I was privileged to have a frame of reference for most of the roadblocks they met because I had been present in the situations they encountered. This enabled me to provide relevant answers to their questions. Homeschooling wasn't without its struggles for both of them or myself, but it was worth it.

I homeschooled both of my children from kindergarten through high school graduation and they both earned scholarships for college. One has now graduated from college and the other is a senior in college. Both are thriving.

You can do it!

Homeschooling can be an incredible gift for you and your children.

Rebecca Black

Learning Language Arts Through Literature

- ◆ Complete integrated program for 1st–12th grades
- ◆ Each level covers: reading, vocabulary, grammar, writing, spelling, and more using real literature
- ◆ Affordable, effective, easy-to-use!

Try four full lessons from each level for free!

Common Sense Press
Simple to teach. Easy to learn.

commonsensepress.com

Award-Winning PreK-12+ Curriculum!

Affordable and easy to use!

FREE Shipping +20% Off!

Visit: www.criticalthinking.com/special-offers

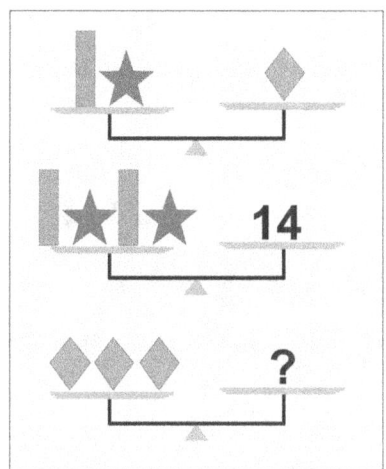

Free Critical Thinking Puzzle of the Week!

Emailed, No Purchase Necessary
Visit:
www.criticalthinking.com/vicki

Homeschool
with Confidence

Vicki Bentley

Exploring Homeschooling:
10 Common Questions

So You've Decided to Homeschool…Now What?
1-hr video "crash course"

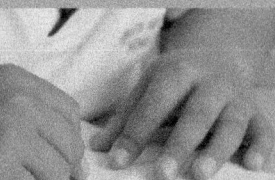

Homeschool Blog Posts

Personal Consultation Services

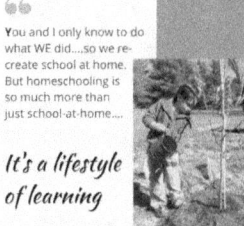

Home Ed 101 books
Mentoring manuals for groups
Parent workbooks for Home Ed 101
Homeschool with Confidence
My Homeschool Planner
Everyday Family Chore System

Home Education 101
6-week online course

Other Online Courses
courses.homeschoolwithconfidence.com

Follow us on Facebook

HWC

www.homeschoolwithconfidence.com
www.everydayhomemaking.com
www.vickibentley.com

Additional Titles From

Sophia Wants to Write a Book

The book kids write themselves! Put your name on the cover. Add your "about the author" photo. Help Sophia write a book and become a real author today.

The Haven: A Light in the Darkness

- Twelve friends
- The world falling apart
- A mission from God

ZamizPress.com Publishing With Integrity

www.ingramcontent.com/pod-product-compliance
Lightning Source LLC
Chambersburg PA
CBHW072016110526
44592CB00012B/1333